IMAGES OF SPORT

GREEN DAYS
CRICKET IN IRELAND
1792–2005

IMAGES OF SPORT

GREEN DAYS
CRICKET IN IRELAND
1792–2005

GERARD SIGGINS

NONSUCH

Front cover: Ed Joyce batting for Ireland during the 2005 ICC Trophy, background is the 1858 All Ireland XI.
Back cover: Angus Dunlop and Kyle McCallan celebrate a wicket during Ireland's C&G Trophy win over Surrey in 2004.

First published 2005

Nonsuch Publishing Limited
The Mill, Brimscombe Port,
Stroud, Gloucestershire, GL5 2QG
www.nonsuch-publishing.com

A catalogue record for this book is available from the National Library.

ISBN 1 84588 512 0

Typesetting and origination by Nonsuch Publishing Limited.
Printed in Great Britain.

Contents

IRELAND

25 miles 50 miles 75 miles

Ramelton • Eglinton • Coleraine
DERRY • Limavady
St Johnston • Ardmore
Strabane • Donemana • Ballymena •
Sion Mills • Carrickfergus •
Bangor •
Ballywater Park
Omagh • **BELFAST** •
Comber
Dungannon • Lisburn • Killinchy
Enniskillen • Lurgan • Waringstown • Gilford • Downpatrick
Armagh •

Castlebar •

Ballyhaunis •

Connemara

Athlone • Dunsany • *Fingal*
Summerhill • Balrothery • Skerries
Ballinasloe • Rush
Malahide
GALWAY •
DUBLIN •
Gort • Kingstown/
Dun Laoghaire
Kildare • Woodbrook
Portlaoise • Bray
Athy •
Roscrea • Avondale
Clarecastle • Nenagh • Castlecomer
Shannon • Carlow
Thurles • Kilkenny •
LIMERICK
Cahir • Carrick-on-Suir
Clonmel • Waterford
Mallow • Fermoy
CORK • Midleton
Innishannon • Cobh
Bandon • Kinsale

**Provincial
structure of
Irish cricket**

North West
North
Connacht
(Comes under
the aegis of the
Munster cricket
union)
Leinster
Munster

Introduction

These are exciting times for Irish cricket, as exciting as they have ever been. This is also an auspicious year: In September 1855, 150 years ago, Ireland played for the first time. In July 2005, Ireland hosted – and almost won – the ICC Trophy for the first time, and can now take its place among the nations of the earth at the 2007 World Cup.

Winning a place in that tournament has made the world take notice of the game here in a way it hasn't done since the West Indies were bowled out for 25 in 1969. The prize money for the ICC Trophy will give unprecedented opportunities to players, coaches and the Irish Cricket Union. Ireland play nine games against county sides in the C&G Trophy in 2006 and a young man from Dublin is set to be the first to emerge from the local game to reach the pinnacle of world cricket.

So full marks to Eoin Purcell from Nonsuch for suggesting this book, which I hope will open many eyes to the depth and breadth of cricket culture in Ireland, and the passion held for a game that has been pursued here for more than two centuries.

There are many people I would like to thank for their help in getting this book into your hands. My passion for cricket and history was bequeathed to me by my father, Brian, and for that and so much else I will be always grateful. My mother, Maureen, doesn't understand or love cricket, but she does understand and love me, and I thank her for that and much, much more. My late cousin, Kieran Hickey, taught me how to love writing and books, and I think about him every time I open one. My wife, Martha and children Jack, Lucy (Railway Union under-11s) and Billy (under-9s) were immensely patient and understanding during the tortuous process. They make every day as exciting, challenging and entertaining as the first day of a Lord's test.

Irish cricket has been well served by those that record its deeds, and I would like to acknowledge and thank Sean Pender, Karl Johnston, Ian Callender, Peter O'Reilly, Philip Boylan, James Fitzgerald, Carl Anderson, Robert Fenton, Peter Breen, Barry Chambers, Emmet O'Riordan, David Townsend, Peter Ball and many un-bylined journalists over the years. Thanks, too, to the unfailingly helpful staff of the Gilbert Library in Pearse Street. Irish cricket literature is thin on the ground, but the magnificent work on Ulster by Clarence Hiles made my job so much easier. Derek Scott's researches into early cricket and his painstaking compilation of the statistics of our game are an immense achievement. Thanks also to the works by Billy Platt, Pat Bell, Colm Murphy, Pat Hone, Michael Milne, Edward Liddle, Dermott Monteith, Neal Garnham and Patrick Bracken for inspiration. Dozens of club publications were consulted and I would like to thank all who laboured on these, and the clubs for permission to quote from them. The ICU newsletters, yearbooks and annuals are a trove of material on the game here and I would like to thank their various editors, including Conor O'Brien, FX Carty, Derek Scott and John Elder. The magazines that came and went have also been useful; thank you to those behind Irish Cricket (1974-75), Irish Cricket Magazine (1984-87), Ulster Cricketer (1985-96, 2004-date) and Irish Cricket Review (1998-99).

My colleagues on The Sunday Tribune have been helpful – and understanding – and I would like to thank Noirin Hegarty, Malachy Clerkin, Paul Howard, Maureen Gillespie and Team Sub for their support. Colm Voyles was a great help with scanning and Paul Lynch with the design of the cover.

Many clubs and individuals gave permission to use photographs from their heritage, for which I am very grateful. Thanks also to Billy Stickland and Inpho for some great modern images. One of Ireland's best batsmen of recent memory, Deryck Vincent, is now playing some fine shots with the camera and I thank him for allowing me to print them.

I talked to many people in the preparation of this book, some of whom preferred to remain uncredited. For all their help and guidance, I thank Derek Scott, Murray Power, Gerry Byrne, Brian Buttimer, Anthony Morrissey, Clarissa Pilkington, Miriam Grealey, Mary Sharp, Michael Sharp, Ed Joyce, John Elder, Michael Halliday, Jason Molins, Ivan Anderson, Philip Boylan, Alan Lewis, Michael Rea Junior, John McGrath, Peter Thompson, Barry Chambers, Deryck Vincent and James Fitzgerald. Thanks also to all those great story tellers of Irish cricket who have related anecdotes on the boundary since I saw my first Ireland game in 1976. James, Murray, Brian and Philip made useful comments at the editing stage which make this a better book than it might have been. However, any errors that have slipped through are my own.

I first got the chance to write about cricket because I set up my own magazine in 1984. It wasn't very good, but it was enormous fun and helped me meet some people who I became privileged to call friends. Anthony Morrissey is only a marginally better cricketer than I, but he never lets me forget it. Michael Dalton was the sort of man that every club needs but few are as lucky as CYM was. His passion for the history of the game was inspirational and his early death in 2003 has left a huge hole in cricket scholarship, and in the lives of all who knew him. I would like to dedicate this book to his memory.

* Gerard Siggins was born in Dublin in 1962. He founded and edited Irish Cricket Magazine (1984-87) and has written on cricket since 1985 in the Sunday Tribune, where he is assistant editor. He is a regular contributor to the CricketIreland website and other publications. He was president of Dublin University CC from 1992-97; for whom his senior career consisted of one match in 1988. He did not bat or bowl, but while fielding stopped one cracking drive by Brian Gilmore. He wishes he had more to say about his cricket career, but is more than happy with that.

gsiggins@tribune.ie
www.historyofirishcricket.com

one

Rising in the
Phoenix

THE GAME of cricket, hewn from fallen branches on the downs of southern England, was carried across the world by its armies and colonial workers. In places like the West Indies, India and Australia, abundant sunlight and long summers ensured that the game took deep root and the masters would eventually bow the knee to their pupils. In Ireland, as in so many other facets of our relationship with England, it wasn't quite that simple.

The Irish climate is, if anything, less suited to the game than in Britain, and while for a time it was the most widely played sport in the country, the Irish have never been able to compete with England – indeed they have never had the chance to do so as equals on the field of play.

It is a sport that has been buffeted more than any other by the turbulent social and political winds of the last two centuries, but it has survived and thrived in several centres and now Irish cricket stands at the brink of a breakthrough with qualification for the 2007 World Cup in the West Indies. How we got there is a remarkable story, and one brightly coloured by some remarkable characters.

The first of these was Oliver Cromwell, Lord Protector to the English and The Butcher of Drogheda to the Irish. What some believe to be the first reference to the game here was in 1656 when Cromwell's Commissioners banned 'Krickett' and burned 'sticks made of ash' and 'balls made of Hollywood'. It is more likely that this was a misidentification of the ancient Irish sport of hurling – cricket bats of the time were curved and resembled the caman – as no more references to cricket have been found to the game being played in Ireland for well over a century after this.

The English historian Rev James Pycroft, in his nineteenth century work The Cricket Field, points out that even when the game was exported, 'Foreigners have rarely, very rarely, imitated us. The English settlers and residents everywhere play cricket; but of no single club have we ever heard dieted with frogs, sauerkraut or macaroni. How remarkable that cricket is not naturalised in Ireland! The fact is very striking that it follows the course of ale rather than whiskey'.

The earliest match in Ireland whose details survive took place in the Fifteen Acres in the Phoenix Park in August 1792, when an eleven of the Garrison played an All Ireland side. One of the names in the Irish side was 'Hon A Wesby', which some authorities believe was a misreading of Arthur Wesley, later Wellesley, later still the Duke of Wellington. Wesley, who was born in what is now the Merrion Hotel in Dublin's city centre, was at the time MP for Trim, County Meath and aide-de-camp to Lord Westmoreland, the King's viceroy in Ireland. Then aged 23, the match report said he 'was also active and remarked for a promising player'.

It is unsurprising that the game was played on a ground adjoining the Viceregal Lodge, for successive viceroys were to play an important role in the development of the game before their departure in 1922 and the renaming of their home as Aras an Uachtarain, now the home of the President. The game was obviously still a novelty to the Irish, as the Journal felt it had to point out that 'the game of Cricket is in England what that of Hurling is in Ireland'. The fixture was arranged a few days earlier at 'a convivial party', when Lieut-Col. Lennox, one of the founders of the Marylebone Cricket Club, threw down a challenge to the Irish which was taken up by the Rt Hon. Major Hobart, Secretary at War. The side bet on the game was the enormous sum of 1,000 guineas.

The 'All Ireland' side was in no way representative of the 4.8 million people then living on the island, being made up almost certainly of a few establishment cronies of Hobart, some of whom may not have even played the game before. Five were MPs in

GARRISON.

Lieut. Col Lennox (35th)	59	B. Cooke
Hon. J. Tufton (33d)	86	Not out
Mr. Reeves (11th)	o	B. Cooke
Mr. Brisbane (38th)	4	C. Emerson
Mr. Abercromby (33d)	o	B. Cooke
Mr. Vaughan (33d)	3	B. Ditto
Mr. Robinson (38th)	1	C. Ditto
Hon. Capt. Douglas (28th)	12	C. Morris
Mr. Wiltshire	28	B. Saunderson
Corporal Battison (35th)	10	B. Cooke
Private Roberts (35th)	14	B. Ditto
Byes	33	
	240	

ALL IRELAND.

Rt. Hon. Maj. Hobart	2	C. Battison	7	C. Tufton
Sec. Cooke	39	B. Lenox	8	B. Wiltshire
Captain Saunderson	1	B. Wiltshire	o	B. Ditto
Hon. A. Wesby	5	B. Lennox	1	C. Battison
Mr. King	o	C. Tufton	10	C. Tufton
Mr. Emerson	4	B. Lennox	10	C. Robinson
Mr. Hickson	o	Run out	11	B. Lennox
Mr. Poyle	o	C. Abercromby	o	C. Wiltshire
Mr. Box	6	C. Robinson	1	C. Brisbane
Simpson	11	C. Tufton	o	B. Lenox
Norris	5	Not out	19	Not out
Byes	3		3	
	76		70	

Thus the gentlemen of the Garrison, it appears, won single hands, by 94 runs.

Above left: The first scorecard. The Freeman's Journal report of the game at the Phoenix Park in 1792.

Above right: The Duke of Wellington, who is believed to have played for All Ireland in the 1792 game. His team-mates that day included *(below left)* Edward Cooke and *(below middle)* Robert Hobart, and they played a Garrison team captained by *(below right)* Charles Lennox.

the Irish House of Commons. Hobart himself was a member of both the English and Irish Commons; from 1789 to 1793 he was Chief Secretary to the Lord Lieutenant of Ireland, and according to his family history 'exerting his influence in this country to prevent any concessions to the Roman Catholics'. He fought a duel with John Philpot Curran, a prominent barrister and defender of Robert Emmet, who courted his daughter Sarah. Hobart was later Governor of Madras and Secretary for War and the Colonies, which role saw the capital of Tasmania named after him.

The game commenced at 1.30pm and the Garrison side were quickly on top. Both opening batsmen, Lennox and Tufton, made fifties and it is likely the score was well past 100 before the first wicket fell. John Tufton batted through the innings for 86 not out, just missing the chance to be immortalised as the first century maker in Ireland. He was to claim his place in cricket history three years later in a game at Moseley in Surrey when he became the first batsman to be given out leg before wicket.

After the fine start, most of the military men struggled to score and the total fell away to 240. It was to be far too much for the Irish XI. The Freeman's Journal reported that, at about four o'clock, 'so keen were the competitors that, without waiting for refreshments, the side of Ireland proceeded upon their Inning'.

Secretary Cooke, who opened the batting with Hobart and scored half Ireland's runs in the first innings, was Edward Cooke, under-secretary at Dublin Castle and of similar political bent to Hobart. The Dublin establishment were very nervous at this time – the game took place just three years after the French revolution, Wolfe Tone had just founded the United Irish Society and a period of armed revolt in Ireland was just around the corner. Cooke was a hardliner; in a report to his minister in London, Cooke wrote that 'I fear relaxation and too much clemency. The snake must be killed – not scotched'. Only one other All Ireland player made double figures and, 'as there was a very great disparity in the number of notches made by the contending parties, the Garrison exceeding Ireland by much, the latter proceeded upon their second INNING', in order that a single day might determine the competition'. That innings was even less successful as the Ireland XI was all out in an hour and a quarter.

The Garrison captain, Lennox, was a major factor in his side's victory. Besides his 59 runs, he 'astonished the spectators with a display of agility and skill during the whole contest, which, even the amateurs of the science admitted to have been without parallel in the course of their experience. His subtlety at bowling it was that so soon caused the event of the day to determine in favour of the Garrison; and his facility of catching the ball may be witnessed, but it cannot be described'.

Lennox was quite a character himself, once fighting a duel with the king's brother, the ('Grand Old') Duke of York, who had accused him of un-gentlemanly behaviour. He was obviously forgiven this act against the royal family and he later assumed the title Duke of Richmond, returning to Ireland as Lord Lieutenant in 1806 with Arthur Wellesley as his secretary. He fought in the Napoleonic wars and observed his old friend's finest hour at Waterloo in 1815, before he was appointed Governor General of Canada where he died of rabies after being bitten in the face by a pet fox. Lennox also played a huge role in cricket history as one of the men who acted as guarantor for Thomas Lord when he opened his first ground at Marylebone in 1787.

The military men pocketed their enormous winnings, and the wife of the Viceroy, Lady Westmoreland, lost the 10 guineas she had bet on Ireland. The Lady was among the spectators less than two months later when a hurling match took place in the park, along with 'several of the nobility and gentry and a vast concourse of spectators'. Such was

Cricket in the Phoenix Park, c. 1830. There were 20 grounds in the Park by 1900 but only two survive. Civil Service play where the game is going on in this painting, while Phoenix play 100 yards further west. (By permission of MCC Library)

the throng that play was eventually abandoned because of encroachment onto the field, despite the endeavours of Lennox.

The social aspect of cricket was early established in Ireland. 'Two handsome marquees were pitched, one in Mr Hobart's shrubbery for the reception of a brilliant circle of ladies of distinction, who graced the simplicity of the manly scene with their presence; the second for the accommodation of the cricket players, on the other side of the Ha Ha in the Fifteen Acres'.

A sport that can last half the waking hours of a day needs to have a social dimension and that has been a strong feature of Irish cricket since that very first day. The rituals of the game have changed little in two centuries: the 'ladies of distinction' obviously remain – many now as players – and the marquees are still pitched for the biggest games. And the venue, Dublin's enormous green lung that is the Phoenix Park, is still an important centre for the sport and two of the oldest clubs. When the military finally withdrew, and the rulers of Dublin Castle handed over the reins of power, Irish cricket was dependent on the clubs for survival, and survive it did.

That game in the Phoenix Park planted a seed, but a few top civil servants, MPs and army officers weren't able to lay down deep foundations for the game in Ireland. For the next forty years there are just a handful of references to cricket in the Irish press, and most of that concerning military sides.

On 11 July 1800 there was a match between the Coldstream Guards and the Third Regiment of Foot Guards at Bandon and a return three weeks later in Kinsale. The first century recorded in Ireland was an innings of 160 by Ensign Beckett for the Coldstreams in one of those games. The board minutes of The King's Hospital school announced in 1803 that soldiers garrisoned in the barracks next to the newly-opened school in Blackhall Place, Dublin, were prohibited from scaling the wall to retrieve their cricket balls. As in England, the game in Ireland expanded after the Napoleonic wars.

There are reports of a side from Avondale setting out to play in Carlow in 1823 and the first documented club was that founded in 1825 in Ballinasloe, Co Galway by Lord Dunlo. The club was active from the late 1820s, but the story of a visit to Kilkenny in 1830 survives chiefly in a song written by the Marquis of Ormonde.

> 'A Club was formed in Garbally,
> The West of Ireland troublin',
> Who said that they beat all the world
> Three years ago in Dublin,
> They swore the Court and Garrison,
> Townspeople and Collegians,
> Could not stand comparison
> With eleven of their Galwegians'

Kilkenny won the match on their own ground on 7 June 1830, and the return match at Dunlo's seat at Garbally too, when the verse was unveiled. It was clearly a triumphal gesture by the south-easterners, who could lay claim to the title of champions of All Ireland.

> 'And now my boys give one cheer more,
> For bat, bails, ball and wicket
> While I propose the three great C's
> Kilkenny, Claret and Cricket.'

Cromwell's commissioners mistaking cricket for hurling was repeated by Amhlaoibh O Suilleabhain, writing in Callan, Co Kilkenny in 1835: 'Ta dha ghne iomana ann, mar ata iomaint ghealach le caman agus liathroid... cricket .i. iomaint ghallda.' (There exist two types of hurling, to wit Irish hurling with a caman and a ball... cricket, that is, foreign hurling...)

A Mr B Phillips, in an article entitled Cricket Fifty Years Ago in the 1879 edition of Lawrence's Handbook of Cricket in Ireland, gave credit to returning students and schoolboys for the spread of the game: 'We can well imagine many an Irish lad as he came home by coach and ship from his English school or university sighing bitterly at the prospective loss of his favourite game'.

Whatever the cause, by 1830 cricket was 'all the rage' in the capital when the Phoenix Park was again at the centre of things. 'The Dublin Club' was formed there in that year, before moving in 1835 to open fields to the south of the Grand Canal at Upper Baggot Street. The earliest members of what became known as Phoenix included a number of gentry, including Lords Dunlo and Clonbrock, who were also members of MCC. In 1838 Phoenix sought the permission of the Commissioner for Woods and Forests to enclose a ground 150 yards square near the Wellington Testimonial, which was given on condition the fence be removed each winter. The following summer saw several players injured on ground that had been badly cut up by horses and cattle and the authorities gave Phoenix permission to permanently enclose the ground.

Cricket had been played in Trinity, usually by English-schooled students, from 1820 or so, but the first evidence for a properly constituted club with officers and a constitution does not emerge until 1835. In the great student tradition of 'any excuse for a party', the club celebrated its 150th anniversary in both 1970 and 1985.

Once the game bedded down, schools became important for introducing boys to cricket. As a sport requiring a certain amount of expenditure and first adopted by the

College Park, 1847. Cricket has been played in Trinity College Dublin from the 1820s to the present day.

upper and middle classes, it was inevitably the elite schools that began to offer cricket to their pupils. A rudimentary form of the game, called 'Stonyhurst cricket' after the public school in Lancashire, was played at Clongowes Wood College in County Kildare as early as 1820. The school began playing against other sides in the 1850s, but persisted in using some odd rules of its own − for example only the long stop was permitted to stop the ball with his coat, and a batsman who played on was deemed 'not out'.

Clongowes developed into the strongest side in the land, taking on the top Dublin clubs and even English public schools. They played Stonyhurst in a two-day match in 1870, and won by two runs. The school was probably the most important nursery for talent in the nineteenth century, with stars such as J.W. Hynes, Montiford Gavin, Tom Ross, Bill Harrington, Dan Comyn and several men called Meldon.

The Irish nationalist leader John Redmond, and his fellow MP brother Willie, took to the game at Clongowes. John was in the XI and was described as 'a steady bat, good fielder and backstop'. One of Redmond's followers in the quest for Home Rule, Tom Kettle, was at the school two decades later. Kettle, who also played for the Malahide club and was a great lover of the game, is best known for the poem he wrote shortly before his death in Flanders in 1916, which he addressed to his daughter Betty:

> 'Know that we fools, now with the foolish dead,
> Died not for the flag, nor King, nor Emperor,
> But for a dream, born in a herdsman's shed,
> And for the secret Scripture of the poor.'

Another Clongowes cricketer better known for his literary exertions was James Joyce, who, according to his brother Stanislaus, 'promised to be a useful bat. He still

College Park, 1861. The Trinity side that year included John Pentland Mahaffy, a future provost, writer and tutor of Oscar Wilde. The large building was the Kildare Street Club, and its windows were reputed to have been broken by a hit from W.G. Grace.

took an interest in the game when he was at Belvedere, and eagerly studied the feats of Ranji, Fry, Trumper and Spofforth'. At the school from 1888 to 1891, Joyce penned a memorable paragraph about cricket there in Portrait of the Artist as a Young Man:

> 'All over the playgrounds they were playing rounders and bowling twisters and lobs. And from here and there came the sounds of the cricket bats through the soft grey air. They said: pick, pack, pock, puck: little drops of water in a fountain slowly falling in the brimming bowl'.

Evidence of the earliest games played by Midleton College, Co Cork survives only from the 1870s but it is likely that the school was playing much earlier as it was also an important source of talent for the new Cork County club in the 1850s. The northern schools seem to have been quicker off the mark, with activity recorded in Portora, Royal School Dungannon and Royal Belfast Academical Institution in the 1840s.

Carlow was to become an important centre of the game for half century after 1831, when the county club was founded at Clogrennan by Horace Rochford. This gentleman, who also founded the All Ireland polo club at the age of 60 in 1873, was an eccentric cricketer to say the least. He bowled very slow, accurate, underarm deliveries, as described by Arthur Samuels in Early Cricket in Ireland:

'He used to commence at least ten yards from the wicket; at every alternate step he would pause and put the ball up to his eye, and so on until he delivered the ball.'

A Lieutenant Lucado, playing for Phoenix, was clearly taking the mickey when he would deliberately walk around the stumps, arriving just in time to receive the ball. Carlow drew players from as far afield as Queen's County (now Laois) and Wicklow before those counties' own clubs were founded. Other clubs that sprang up in this first expansion of the game included Desart, Diamor, Maryborough (Portlaoise) and Avondale, which was founded by John Parnell, father of a man later known as 'The Uncrowned King of Ireland', Charles Stewart Parnell. Parnell senior played for Cambridge University in 1831 (going in at No 9 he top scored with 22), and retained a life-long interest in the game. A life-terminating interest too, as playing against his doctor's advice for County Wicklow in the Phoenix Park in 1859, he took a turn and died the next day in the Shelbourne Hotel, aged 48.

His illustrious son played the game regularly as a boy for Avondale and later for Magdalene College while at Cambridge. On graduation he returned home and played for County Wicklow for a decade as a useful all-rounder. Worse players than he were capped at the time. Parnell played for Phoenix for a time, but an 1866 committee meeting complained that he had not paid his subscription. By 1875, when he was elected MP for Meath, his cricketing life was at an end. His turbulent career saw him rise to the leadership of the Irish Parliamentary Party, enduring a scandal in which his signature was forged on letters condoning political murders, and finally being embroiled in a nasty divorce involving his mistress Kitty O'Shea. He died in 1891 aged just 45.

According to an 1898 biography by Richard Barry O'Brien, Parnell was quick to show his temper on the cricket field. On one occasion his County Wicklow side travelled up by horse and carriage to the Phoenix Park. Shortly after play commenced Parnell became embroiled in a row with the Phoenix captain. Rather than back down – as encouraged to do by his team-mates – Parnell led his team from the field and play was abandoned. If one considers the 50 mile journey made by his side he must have been quite unpopular on the trip home.

Back in the 1830s Kilkenny continued their triumphs – they beat Ballinasloe twice more, and also chalked up wins over Carlow and Maryborough before travelling up to Dublin to play a strong combined side of Phoenix and the Garrison in July 1835. The county side won by an innings, but the strength of Dublin cricket at the time was shown the following week when the new Queen's County club also beat Dublin/Phoenix by an innings! The game continued to develop in the south, with the military to the fore. In Clarecastle in 1832, the officers and men of the thirty-second regiment of Light Infantry played for a prize of £50 donated by the officers. In the same year the Clare Cricket Club promoted a play and concert. A letter to the Tipperary Free Press in June 1834 announcing the formation of the Carrick-on-Suir club on land 'kindly given' by Mr H. Mandeville and the following year a club from Roscrea visited Carlow, beating Rochford's club by two wickets. The largest county, Cork, had several important garrison towns and it was in these that the game took root. There were active military sides from the beginning of the eighteenth century, with games being played in Mallow, Fermoy, Bandon, Kinsale and Cobh.

In the north of the island, where in the twenty-first century the playing numbers are greatest, it was much slower to get off the ground. In 1828 the Belfast News Letter referred to a private match against Killyleagh at Killinchy, County Down. The first club to form was Belfast Cricket Club in 1830, but it wasn't until the formation of

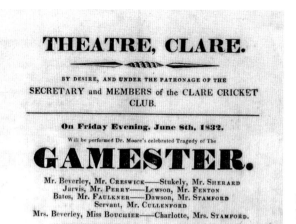

Handbill for a theatrical event promoted by Clare Cricket Club, 1832 (courtesy Clare County Library).

Lisburn (1836) and the Ulster Club (1839) that they played 'outside' games. There was a keen rivalry between Belfast and Ulster, and the Northern Whig of 1st September 1840 reported on a low scoring game at Lagan Bridge. Ulster made 23 and 50 to Belfast's 23 and 24, but the newspaper hints at some tension: 'We hear that (Belfast) attribute their reverse to the circumstance that three excellent players (Messrs Stuart, Thursby and Woodgate, officers of the Eighty-sixth) whom they did not, at the time of making the match, know to be members of the opposing club, were ranged against them.' The use of imported 'hired guns' has been a controversial issue for much of the two centuries since!

   Throughout the nineteenth century there were between 20,000 and 30,000 British troops garrisoned in Ireland, and they proved an important impetus to the development of sport, particularly soccer and cricket. Their presence was not always a divisive one, even with the increase in armed rebellion in the second half of the century. The arrival of the railways in 1834 revolutionised trade and travel between the towns and cities of Ireland. Cricket was facilitated, too, by this improved communication, and by 1840 there were dozens of clubs around the country. The game was ripe for take off.

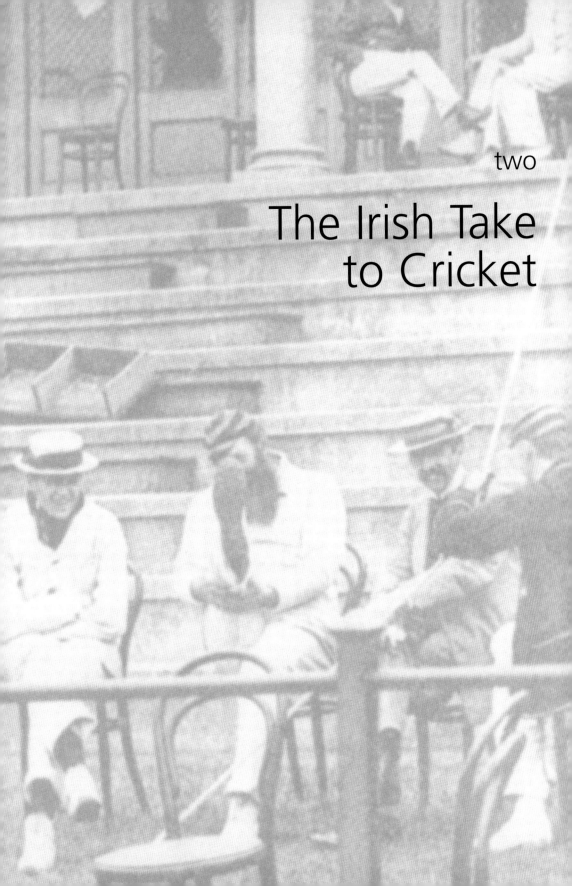

two

The Irish Take
to Cricket

The 1840s were a troubled decade in Ireland, with famine and insurrection casting a long shadow, but cricket continued to expand, with new clubs springing up in places such as Cahir (1841), Bandon (1843), Roebuck (1844), Kingstown (1848), Castlecomer, Clonmel and Downpatrick (1849). The potato famine of 1845-49, which claimed the lives of approximately one million people, also saw a similar number flee the country, setting off a wave of emigration which meant the population continued to decrease for the next century. Ironically, many of the diaspora took to the game in their new homelands – not counting Ireland games, more than 120 Irishmen played first-class cricket around the world – and Ireland's emigrants gave cricket such greats as Bill O'Reilly, Glenn McGrath and Jason Gillespie (Australia), Cuan McCarthy (South Africa) and Martin Donnelly (New Zealand).

While cricket claimed participants across the social spectrum, especially outside the cities, it was still essentially a pastime of the upper and middle classes, who were not as badly affected by the famine. Indeed, the seeds for the game's decline in some parts may have been sown by the leisured and ostentatious approach of the likes of the Nenagh club whose annual dinner was described in the local newspaper in 1849: 'the dinner, viands, etc, were all of the best description and served up with the order and regularity for which this well-known establishment is proverbial'.

The county of Cork, which hosted several important garrisons, had seen plenty of cricket before 1850, but the laying down of the pitch on the Mardyke in that year was to provide a spiritual home to the Munster game that still holds. The club at Queen's College (now University College Cork) was founded in 1849 and for many years the season opened with a game between the students and the Cork City club.

The game in Ulster, after a slow start, was starting to flourish. Three important clubs that were to dominate the game in the north were founded in the 1850s: Waringstown (1851), North Down (1857) and North of Ireland (1859). Further clubs followed with the growth of the linen trade as mill owners provided grounds for workers such as at Sion Mills and Donacloney. The expansion of the railway network after the first track was laid in Dublin in 1834, and Belfast in 1839, facilitated cheap and speedy travel between towns and helped spread the game all over the provinces.

The most important developments were taking place in Dublin, however, and a Londoner called Charles Lawrence was at the centre of things. There had been early contests with English sides – Phoenix travelled to Liverpool in 1839 and I Zingari came to Dublin in 1851 – but it was the contacts Lawrence had built up in England, and his keenness to augment his income, that saw an upsurge in contact between cricketers of the neighbouring islands. Lawrence had played for Middlesex and Surrey and played an important role in the development of the game in Scotland and Australia as well as Ireland. In 1849 he took all ten wickets for Scotland against the All England XI. In May 1851 he arrived in Dublin to take up a post as professional with Phoenix CC. There were few big games on the Dublin calendar to tantalise Lawrence, and his entrepreneurial streak saw him organise visits in 1853 by the MCC (Phoenix lost by 79 runs) and the United England XI (The 22 men of Phoenix won by an innings and 105 runs), but his greatest idea was to set up the All Ireland XI.

In much the same way as the professional elevens took the game to the towns of England, Lawrence's side played on a commercial basis and toured the island taking on teams for agreed stakes and helping further popularise cricket. He rode the rail building boom, particularly with the completion of the Dublin-Belfast line in 1853. Unfortunately for Lawrence there was insufficient demand for his product and he never did make his fortune.

Ireland v I Zingari at the Vice-Regal Lodge, 1866. Ireland bowled the English touring side out for 33 and 42 to win by 151 runs. J.P. Mahaffy took 9-16 in the first innings.

It is not known whether Lawrence had any hand in organising the 1855 fixture between Ireland and the Gentlemen of England, which has been accepted by the Irish Cricket Union as the first representative game (although the union was not proposed until 1884 and selectors not appointed until a body was finally formed in 1890). Ireland was victorious in this game, 96 and 105 against the visitors 56 and 38, which was played at Phoenix on 10-11 September. At least eight of the Irish side were members of the host club but few of the English side seem to have been leading players, only three playing for the Gentlemen in other matches that summer. One, a Cambridge student called R.A. Fitzgerald, went on to be one of the most powerful administrators as Secretary of MCC and also played for Ireland.

The following season the Gentlemen of England returned to Phoenix, this time winning by 39 runs, despite fifty and ten wickets by Charles Lawrence. He was again to the fore when the United All England XI came to Phoenix in September 1856. The English side was packed with top professionals, notably Lillywhite, Caffyn, Lockyer, Grundy and Wisden so Ireland agreed to field 18 players in opposition. These 'odds' matches were common in the nineteenth century. The Irish side included two professionals, Lawrence and Peter Doyle, but the side mainly comprised Phoenix and Trinity men. The 18 mustered 116 all out in the first innings, with 22 by old Etonian William Johnston the top score. Joseph McCormick, Liverpool-born captain of Cambridge University, was the star of the show for Ireland with the ball, taking 6-48 as the Englishmen built a small lead of ten runs. John Wisden, founder of the most famous sporting annual, took seven wickets for the second time as Ireland collapsed to 71 all out leaving the visitors to get just 62 to win. McCormick and Lawrence bowled more than

Above left: George Frith Barry, who was given a post in the Dublin Castle administration by the cricket-loving Viceroy the Earl of Carlisle.

Above right: Rev. Joseph McCormick, who played in the first five games for Ireland.

Below: David Trotter from Summerhill, County Meath. Trotter was the first Irishman to score a century against professional opposition. He played for North v South in London in 1877.

70 overs unchanged as the visitors struggled to master the conditions and despite 18 by Wisden they were all out for 55, six runs short.

Heartened by this display, Lawrence received a significant boost when the Lord Lieutenant, Queen Victoria's representative in Ireland, asked him to build a cricket field for him on the grounds of his lodge in the Phoenix Park. The 7th Earl of Carlisle was an eccentric bachelor who, although he was no player, was a great lover of the game. He liked nothing better than to potter across to Phoenix and keep the scorebook. He was a great patron of the game, founded the Civil Service club in 1863 and his name lived on in the name of a senior Dublin club until the 1990s, albeit second hand – the Carlisle club took their name from a street where their early members lived. In 1862 he opened the Bray Athletic Cricket and Archery Ground, but it was later popularly abbreviated to 'The Carlisle Grounds'.

The Earl provided Lawrence with a fine, if small, ground on his lawn in the Phoenix Park and allowed him to organise a benefit match for his efforts. Lawrence had the field surrounded by canvas walls to allow him charge admission but the day turned foul and the barriers were blown away. Lawrence lost money on the match but Carlisle gave him the facilities once more to save him from bankruptcy.

The Vice-Regal ground – dodgy outfield but the best square in Ireland – became the centre of the game for the elite of what was known as the second city of the Empire. Carlisle's imprimatur encouraged many aspiring gentlemen to take up and patronise the sport and the games at the lodge became tremendously important social occasions. Carlisle hosted one or two games a week, and he invariably spent the whole day in the scorekeepers' tent. The highlight was usually the game against I Zingari, a wandering club usually comprised of the moneyed echelons of English society, whose members were put up by in the Vice-Regal Lodge.

The Vice-Regal side was more egalitarian. A leading Irish player from the 1840s to the 1860s, Arthur Samuels, recalled that the best batsmen were his Lordship's coachman, butler and baker. Samuels also wrote about a game he played for Phoenix against Vice-Regal. A Captain Munday had bragged to him before the game that he had never been bowled by an underarm bowler, of which style Samuels was a prime exponent. 'If you bowl me, I will present you with this special gold watch and chain', he scoffed. Sure enough, Samuels knocked over Munday's middle stump with the first ball he bowled. 'The shouting and cheering that arose from his friends in the Pavilion was deafening. The next and last I saw of the captain was when he was driving away from the ground five minutes later; but he quite forgot to leave the watch and chain for me; he was marked 'absent' in the second innings.'

Lawrence continued to organise high profile games against professional and top class opposition. With Peter Doyle he organised a series of Gentlemen v Players games, but they were not as successful as their equivalent in England which were the highlight of the summer in pre-international times. A side calling itself the Gentlemen of England played Ireland at the Rotunda Gardens in 1857, though again this was not a true representative side. Only one of the team played for Gents v Players that season – as did Ireland's all rounder McCormick. Lawrence was again dominant (46, 14 and eight wickets), with McCormick also to the fore (4, 56 and 5 wickets) as the visitors escaped with a draw.

Lawrence was quite a sporting pioneer, also opening a tennis court as a commercial venture. This failed, the Irish not being quite ready for the game and it was another 15 years before the first tennis clubs were founded. Lawrence's finest hour for Ireland came at the home of cricket, Lord's, in May 1858. Ireland took on a decent MCC side, every

Gentlemen of Ireland in the Phoenix Park, 1858. This was only the sixth game played by Ireland and the earliest team group to survive. The team that played against Birkenhead Park was: G.F. Barry, T. Quin, P. Doyle, Capt Hon. W. Edwardes, J.W. Greene, C. Lawrence, Capt J. Coddington, J. Roberts, Major Boothby, R. Cooke, A. Samuels.

one of whom played some first-class cricket, and won by an innings and ten runs. The game was played in poor weather conditions – 'thick mud' according to Lawrence – and the first day's crowd was sparse. Lawrence bowled unchanged as MCC collapsed to 53 all out, the Londoner taking 8-32 from his 23 overs. Doyle and Tom Quinn batted out till tea, when further rain put the end to play with Ireland 19-0. The weather was better on day two, and a large crowd turned up to watch, including Carlisle and his party. The openers were soon dismissed but McCormick rattled up 34 and Hon. Spencer Ponsonby 18 to give Ireland a respectable 120. McCormick (5-27) and Lawrence (4-25) shared the 63 overs of the MCC innings and saw them off for 57. Lawrence took his All Ireland XI to play in Belfast and Scotland, but he probably decided the writing was on the wall when Carlisle was replaced as Lord Lieutenant by Lord Eglington in 1858.

I Zingari were regular visitors, usually accompanied by the MCC Secretary, R.A. Fitzgerald, who played several times for Ireland. 'Fitz' saw the visits as a way of bridging the gap between Ireland and the English:

> 'Whatever little difference may exist between certain sections of Shillelagh worshippers and her most Gracious Majesty, under whose oppressive rule we hope to bow our neck, there can be no question about the unanimity that prevails between the willow wielders, Celt and Sassenach'.

An Irish equivalent to I Zingari, who adopted the cod-Irish name 'Na Shuler', were formed in 1863 by members of the gentry. They continued until the Great War, playing annually at the likes of Ballywalter Park, County Down and Castle Bandon, County Cork. Their spirit was reborn in 1948 with the Leprechauns club, who tour the south-east every summer and turn out many sides against school teams.

There were two visits in the early 60s by very strong All England XIs, and Ireland were well beaten on each occasion. Willsher (16 for 52) and Tinley (23 for 83) ran through the Irish XXII twice for 70 and 83 at Rathmines, while top batters Julius Caesar, Richard Daft, Tom Hayward and George Parr knocked up the runs. At the Coburg Gardens in Dublin (next to the modern National Concert Hall) in 1861, Ireland was again bowled out twice for less than a hundred. Later that summer J Davidson became the first northern cricketer to play for Ireland on a trip to Scotland. It would be another 73 years before a north-westerner would get the call-up.

Lawrence left Phoenix for Australia in 1861 as a member of H.H. Stephenson's touring side, staying on and playing for New South Wales. Lawrence returned to the UK as a manager of the Aboriginal touring team in 1868, but these exotic tourists never came to Ireland. According to historian and former test spinner Ashley Mallett, 'perhaps he more than any other person could claim the title of the Father of Australian cricket'. And more than any other, he was probably Father of Irish cricket too.

Lawrence's departure left the way open to other entrepreneurs, and the clubs themselves filled the gap. Improved travel links with Britain and professional sides willing to journey far and wide for a purse meant Ireland became a regular stop on their circuit. Leinster were the first to host the greatest cricketer of all, W.G. Grace, in 1873, while North, the wealthiest club in Ulster, also had the wherewithal to bring over his XI in 1875.

College Park in Dublin became the centre of Irish cricket, with the student club promoting fixtures against top English opposition virtually every season from 1870 to the outbreak of the First World War. The city centre location and Trinity's importance in Victorian society ensured a great attendance – at times exceeding 5,000 – each summer

The Mardyke, Cork, 1856. A watercolour by Bosanquet.

and allowed the students to test their skills against the best of the English amateurs and professionals, as well as Australia (in 1880 and 1905) and South Africa (1894, 1901 and 1904). As late as 1923 the college side played the West Indies.

But the showpiece fixtures were just the icing on the cake: the game itself was in great health throughout the 1860s. More clubs sprang up all over the country and, according to Samuels 'had taken such a hold that it was patronised by all classes'. By 1869 the Lawrence annual was able to report that there were clubs in every county except Donegal, Kerry, Limerick and Roscommon. By 1871 those gaps had been filled and it was now a 32 county game. (In the twenty-first century there are clubs in every county except Monaghan, Cavan, Sligo, Leitrim and Longford). The county of Tipperary, where the game these days is played by just one small, if thriving, club in Ballyeighan, was the centre of a busy cricket scene. Patrick Bracken's Foreign and Fantastic Field Sports details how the county played host to dozens of clubs, peaking at 43 in 1876.

The Ireland side continued playing two or three times a season, notching up wins against MCC at Lord's in 1862 and 1868. The London Times, reporting the latter game, said that Ireland won 'much to the astonishment of the spectators and, I must say, to the delight of many'. The Times reporter became carried away with the importance of the result:

> 'There were now 101 runs to get before the haughty Saxon should acknowledge himself humbled; and, as belonging to neither country, or, more properly, to both, we are bound to say that we never saw a more gallant struggle, and the iniquities of several hundred years of oppression and wrong are now indelibly wiped out.'

The professional elevens became frequent visitors to Dublin, usually playing 22 Irishmen and beating them comfortably. One Irishman was able to compete on equal terms, however – a lad called David Trotter from Summerhill, County Meath. Until this century Trotter was the youngest Irish international, aged just 17 years, 115 days when he played against I Zingari in 1875. The following season, playing for Dublin University, he scored 109 against a United South of England XI captained by W.G. Grace. This stunning innings – the first century by an Irishman against professional opposition – was noticed in England and when he made a hundred against Birkenhead Park and 77 against the MCC at Lord's, he was selected in 1880 for the North of England to play the South. Trotter did well enough – 9 and 33 – but his side lost by an innings thanks to Grace's 261.

Other Irishmen were making their mark abroad. Tom Horan, born in Midleton, County Cork, played for Australia in the first ever test match in 1877, and later became Australia's leading cricket journalist. Waterford-born Thomas Kelly played in the second and third matches, playing against a fellow Irishman in the latter game in January 1879. Leland Hone, one of an important Irish cricketing family, had been chosen to tour Australia under Lord Harris in 1878-79 after just two first-class appearances, both for MCC against the universities. Although selected as a middle-order batsman, it became apparent that Harris had neglected to bring a regular wicketkeeper and so Hone was drafted in, playing in the only Test against Australia at Melbourne.

By the early 1880s all was not well in Ireland, and cricket was to suffer more than any other sport. Ironically, it was Parnell, the Avondale star, who was to set in train the process of decline. He was first elected MP for Meath in 1875, and two years later took over as leader of the Home Rule Party. In 1879 Parnell helped found the Land League, whose campaign for fair rent, free sale and fixity of tenure almost immediately caused a huge split between landlord and tenant. In the rural counties, where cricket was played largely under the patronage of landlords, the land war was devastating for the game.

Allied to the upsurge in nationalism sparked by the Fenians and the growth in interest in the Gaelic games of hurling and football, cricket's role as a social glue was weakened and rapidly turned to dust.

In 1884 the Gaelic Athletic Association was founded in Thurles, County Tipperary, but by then cricket's decline was well advanced. With society being increasingly polarised, cricket's association with England and the aristocracy cost it many adherents. The GAA's infamous ban on foreign sports was not to blame – that piece of nastiness was the work of the second generation of officials in the 1890s and early 1900s – but it put the final nail in the coffin of the game in many areas. The tensions engendered by the increased nationalism took their toll too, as this report from Blackwoods Magazine in 1887 suggests:

> 'The late Earl of Carlisle, when Lord Lieutenant of Ireland, did well by bringing 12 over to play in the Phoenix Park, and to visit several county clubs, but their colours caused them to be hooted and pelted by 'wearers of the green' in the wilder districts: and if such was the spirit in the halcyon days of Eglington and Abercorn, it is to be feared that now little cricket intercourse will take place with Ireland.'

Even in the cities the atmosphere was changing and there were a lot more attractions for athletic young men. Arthur Samuels complained that the Kingstown (later Dun Laoghaire) club which scored victories over Phoenix, the Military and the University, broke up when they found it hard to get the locals to practise because 'the attractions of the bands on the pier and other allurements carried them away'.

Lawrence's annual complained that the new Lord Lieutenant had 'all but closed' the Vice-Regal Lodge to the game, with just the visit of MCC in 1879. 'His grace prefers offering a tempting lure to the Salmonidae rather than alluring a too confident batsman to step out to slows'.

Perhaps the example of cricket showed the entrepreneurs that there was money to be made from the increased leisure time available. Henry Dunlop founded the Irish Champion Athletic Club and in 1873 secured a plot of land at Lansdowne Road in Dublin where he organised clubs for athletics, cycling, tennis, rugby as well as cricket. All the new sports became popular and ate into the constituency for cricket, further reduced when golf took off in the late 1880s. Cricket is not a simple game to organise – it requires getting at least 24 people together at one time, a well-prepared ground and expensive equipment. Golf, for example, is a game that can be played with much smaller numbers, even on one's own. Football and rugby are far less expensive to organise and play. But the changed political climate was probably most to blame. The last edition of the Lawrence Annual – driven out of business by declining interest in the game – pointed the finger.

> 'It was not to be expected that in 1880 and 1881 – when Ireland was passing through a political and commercial crisis – our noble game should have escaped the universal depression. Here in Ireland, cricket is unfortunately not the pastime of the masses, as it is in England… we must look more to the aristocracy and the well-to-do commercial class for our votaries, and unfortunately these are the very classes most seriously affected financially by the unfortunate circumstances through which the country has been passing.'

For all these reasons, the game of cricket declined from the pre-eminence it held in Irish sport in the 1870s. In some areas it disappeared as quickly as it had flourished, while outside Dublin and the protestant communities in the North it rapidly became a minority sport, a status it has never been able to shake off to this day.

Above left: W.G. Grace jokes for the camera, College Park 1898. Grace visited Ireland seven times to play cricket.

Above right: Thomas Horan from Midleton, County Cork, who played in early test matches for Australia.

three

American
Adventures

of Irish Gentlemen · vs · Gentlemen of Philadelphi

MANHEIM ✳ 1892 ✳

With so many Irishmen and women having fled hunger and poverty for the United States, it was natural that some links between the cricket community would be maintained with those who had left. Two New York lawyers, including Edward Moeran, a Cork-born Trinity graduate who helped found NICC, were members of the St George's club and organised the invitation for the Gentlemen of Ireland to visit America in 1879. It was an extraordinarily ambitious tour, the first of four such trips over the next thirty years.

It was a strong side that left Kingsbridge station on 31 August, waved off by a large party including the Lord Mayor of Dublin, with their luggage stamped with a green crest that read 'The All Ireland Eleven'. All of the party were members of Phoenix, but club affiliation was somewhat looser in those days and Phoenix held a place in Irish cricket approximate to that of MCC in England. The side was led by Nathaniel Hone, who brought with him his two cousins William and Jeffrey, and his brother William 'The General', who regarded the trip as a honeymoon for he and his recently-acquired wife and played little cricket. A terrible tragedy struck the Hone family two years later when Nathaniel's nephew, Nat junior, died from drinking acid wrongly sold to him as medicine in a Limerick chemist while on a cricket tour with Na Shuler. Nat, who was just 20, had played for Cambridge University that summer and would surely have gone on to play for Ireland as seven other members of the family did.

The rest of the party was David Trotter, Sir George Colthurst, Horace Hamilton, Jack Nunn, Arthur Exham, Charles Barrington, Rowley Miller, George Casey, Hugh Gore and Henry Brougham. The story of the tour survives chiefly thanks to Brougham, who wrote a lively account of the tour entitled: *The Irish Cricketers in the United States 1879, by One*

Above left: Dominic Cronin, elected captain for the 1892 tour on the voyage out.

Above right: Believed to be the earliest photograph of an Ireland game: a scene from the 1888 game against Philadelphia.

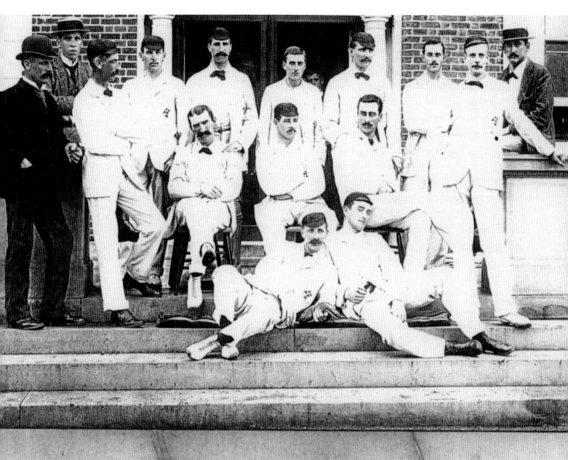

Mr Meldon's Eleven of Irish Gentlemen · vs · Gentlemen of Philadelphia
*MANHEIM * 1892*

Ireland v Philadelphia, Manheim 1892. – the touring party was J.W. Hynes, J.M. Meldon, M. Gavin, B.B. Hamilton, A. Penny, W. Vint, E.R. Thompson, F.F. Kilkelly, G.C. Green, W.F. Thompson, T.I. Considine and C.L. Johnson. The manager was Capt. D. Rutledge and H.J. Daly the scorer. Johnson, who later played tests for South Africa, is wearing the boater, second from the left.

of Them'. This rare booklet tells the story of their travels around what was a strange and unknown land. Their encounter with black people was obviously a novel experience:

> 'The waiters were all niggers as black as coal. They were fine-looking men, and once we found that the black of their hands did not come off on the plates – a feeling that was very strong amongst us at first – we agreed that niggers were excellent servants.'

Some of the party were clearly unimpressed with the spectacular sights they saw. One, on seeing Niagara Falls, remarked 'Arra, sure why wouldn't it fall, what's to hinder it?'

The opposition was mixed, with some mismatches resulting. Ireland struggled to make 57 all out against Central New York, but the eighteen men of the hosts could only make 16 and 38 between them, with Horace Hamilton ending up with the remarkable analysis 16-4-13-13 and Arthur Exham 31.2-8-23-12. The New York Daily Courier reported that 'The Irish Cricketers gave the Americans what Paddy gave the drum – a bad beating.'

The game in America's largest city was not as strong as it was in Philadelphia, where there were thirty clubs. The first game against Germantown saw the Irish go down by an innings but they recovered to beat a United Philadelphia XI by two wickets, the game hinging on a mistaken call of 'not out' by Arnold Rylott, the Irish umpire. The party had debated whether they would play Rylott, a Leicestershire professional who was employed by Phoenix. The consensus was not to use him and he spent the trip as umpire. The next game against the Young America club was called off when the hosts refused to accept Rylott as umpire. They insisted they did not question his good faith but that 'in a match amongst gentlemen, gentlemen must umpire'. The Irish stood by their man and the game was called off. The last leg of the tour took the team to Canada, where Hamilton broke the Canadian pole vault record!

Nine years later another tour was organised, although none of Hone's party travelled this time. Most of the leading players of the day were unavailable, including Trotter, the three Hamilton brothers and David Emerson. The 13-man party was made up mainly of students or recent graduates from Trinity, with the addition of Thomas Tobin of Leinster, and Daniel Gillman and Captain John Dunn of Phoenix. Dunn was an Australian-born military man who had taken Irish cricket by storm, scoring six centuries in a week in the summer of 1887. He played a bit for Surrey and MCC, but after being posted to the Far East he drowned along with most of his Hong Kong team-mates when the SS Bokhara sank returning from their annual match with Shanghai in 1892.

The 1888 tour was organised by John Hynes, aged just 23, and captained by Dominic Cronin, who was elected by the players on the journey out. The tour manager was Thomas Lyle from Coleraine, a rugby international. Hynes had a great tour, scoring 500 runs at 28 and taking 78 wickets at 7. The team remained unbeaten on the Canadian leg, winning the three-day international by an innings. The Americans were stronger, and after a five run win in Boston they travelled on to Philadelphia. This game was a most exciting affair, with Ireland chasing 127 to win in the fourth innings. At 87 for six it was still anyone's game but wickets fell steadily and the tourists needed 14 to win when last man Tobin walked to the wicket. Walked may not be an accurate term, as according to reports 'Before he went into bat, Tobin received many tonics, both physical and spiritual and fortified by the drinks, went to the wicket.' He was clearly in no state to bat, and taking evasive action to the first ball he faced, fell over and scrambled back to his ground on all fours! The next ball demolished his stumps and Philadelphia had won by seven runs.

A three-day match followed against All New York, where Dunn scored 126 as Ireland won by nine wickets but the tour ended with a 39-run defeat in Philadelphia with just two minutes to go. Again Tobin was the unfortunate last man – a late order collapse meant he was rushed out to the wicket without pads or gloves. He was out first ball. Four years later Hynes was off Stateside again, this time under the captaincy of Jack Meldon, the only other survivor from the 1888 tour. Meldon, who was a teenager on the previous tour, led a weak party. Most of the top Irish cricketers of the day were unavailable or unwilling to travel, including a chastened Tobin, Frank Browning, Lucius Gwynn and Timothy O'Brien, who although born in Baggot Street in Dublin was then

GENTLEMEN OF IRELAND CRICKET TEAM.

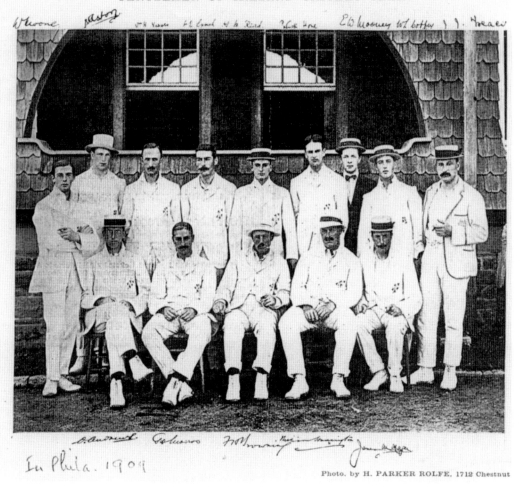

Gentlemen of Ireland party, Philadelphia 1909.   Back row: W. McMooney, J.G. Aston, W.H. Napper, J.E. Lynch, H.M. Read, W.P. Hone, E. McMooney, W.L. Coffey, J.J. Treacy; Front: O. Andrews, G.A. Morrow, F.H. Browning, W. Harrington, J.M. Magee.

a leading county batsman with Middlesex and test player with England. The Irish squad included William Vint, a classy wicketkeeper from Belfast who was the first man to score 1,000 runs in a season for NICC, in 1875. He later emigrated Down Under where he played for Victoria, taking part in the first century stand for the 10th wicket in Australia. The party left Dublin after a farewell dinner in a Ringsend rowing club but the journey across the Atlantic was fraught. Clem Johnson (later to play tests for South Africa) and Archie Penny were sick for the entire 11-day voyage, while Johnson was almost swept overboard in a storm. Rain ruined the Canadian leg of the tour, but Ireland chalked up a good win in New York where they made 203 to win on the final day.

On they went to Philadelphia for a three-match series against the local selection, the

J.M. Meldon: played for Ireland from 1888 to 1910.

first of which was won by 127 runs, Ireland's first triumph over the leading American side. More than 15,000 people turned up for the second day's play which saw Montiford Gavin carry his bat for an unbeaten 90. Meldon (81) and Penny (59 not out) also made important runs in this landmark result. The second game was lost, thanks to 10 wickets by the American star Bart King, and the third game was drawn. Honours ended even, a most satisfactory result for the tourists.

The Philadelphians visited Ireland in 1907 and extended an invitation to tour for the fourth time. On 28 July 1909 the Committee Controlling Cricket in Ireland met at the Metropole Hotel in Dublin to pick a party to tour North America. The Philadelphians had agreed to defray expenses and organised seven games. Frank Browning was elected captain on the voyage out from Liverpool and after two minor games in Canada moved onto Staten Island for a game against All New York. Bill Harrington and William Napper opened the bowling and soon had six Americans back in the pavilion without a run on the board! The New Yorkers 'recovered' to 29 all out, with Napper returning 6-21 and Harrington 4-7. Browning made 30 as Ireland took a lead of 98, and Napper was once again lethal, finishing with 6-88 as he dismissed the hosts for 177. George Morrow made an unbeaten 33 as Ireland won by nine wickets.

The Philadelphians at the time were very strong, and won both of the major matches by an innings and plenty. King was unplayable, taking all ten Irish wickets (seven clean bowled) as they collapsed to 111 all out, with only the opener Morrow unbeaten on 50 – although he had been bowled by a no-ball from King. White made a century for the Americans as they racked up 353 and King was again to the fore, taking a hat-trick (bowling Morrow, Browning and Aston), as Ireland were dismissed for 74. He took 11 more wickets in the second match, finishing the two-game series with 25 at 6.04. King is regarded as the greatest American cricketer of all time, and one who did well against greater sides than Ireland. In three tours to England, he took 238 wickets in just 38 games with his fast bowling which could swing both ways.

The American tours were good for Irish cricket, helping to blood several young players and giving them a taste of adventure. With the decline and fall of Philadelphian cricket there were no more invitations and Ireland reduced its touring ambitions for the next sixty years to the neighbouring island.

four

Getting Organised

Although Phoenix and Trinity had taken the lead in forging links with England, there were other clubs all over the island who were keen to test themselves on and off the field. North of Ireland, founded in November 1859 at a meeting in the Royal Hotel in Donegall Place, rapidly developed into the leading club in the region, at one stage boasting more than 200 members and nine professionals. They certainly hit the ground running, as the season after their foundation they hosted the All England XI in a three-day match at their grounds on the Ormeau Road. 'Twenty of the North of Ireland club and Ground, with Two Bowlers' were only 18 behind the visitors on first innings but lost by six wickets. That first season saw North secure a ground, build a pavilion at a cost of £433, and stage a tour in England!

The game took root in the North-West later than anywhere else, and became organised much more slowly, but that may be due to the village-based nature of much of the cricket in the area, chiefly the counties of Derry and Tyrone but also including Fermanagh and Donegal. In much the same way that the GAA developed on a parish basis, North-West allegiances were defined by pride in the village and many of the most powerful sides ever since have been based in small settlements such as Sion Mills and Donemana. There is evidence of cricket in the Derry area in 1847, and there were clubs formed at Newtownlimavady (1856) and Sion Mills (1864), but according to Clarence Hiles's A History of Senior Cricket in Ulster, it was the arrival and extension of the railway network that facilitated rapid growth. Villages developed trading links with Derry and cricketing links followed. Sion Mills reputedly holds the record for the longest hit in cricket history when the ball landed in the goods wagon of a passing train and was transported to Derry, 17 miles away!

The first edition of Lawrence's Handbook of Cricket in Ireland in 1865 reviews only three sides in the north-western counties – Limavady CC and the Royal Schools at Dungannon, County Tyrone and Portora, Enniskillen, County Fermanagh, although the latter played and beat Raphoe, County Donegal in the preceding season. Sion Mills, for many years the strongest side in the region, flourished under the patronage of the Herdman family who were prosperous millowners. The family created the settlement as a 'model village' in the 1830s – no public house was allowed until a court battle in 1897 – and its eccentric 15th century English architecture is preserved by a trust. The small ground in the shadow of Herdman's mill has seen many epic battles, none more famous than the 1969 international against West Indies in which the visitors were bowled out for 25, a result which made the name of the tiny County Tyrone village known the world over. The linen mill finally closed in 2004 and its production moved to South Africa.

Back in Dublin, the prosperous suburbs just south of the city centre were home to a Bal-ballon club in the 1850s. This obscure French sport was a temporary craze which captivated dozens of young men and women before going the way of all crazes. 'Some of the young blades of the time did not consider the game spirited enough', wrote one observer, so the game of cricket was adopted to up the adrenaline of the members. Thus the famous Leinster Cricket Club was formed in Rathgar on 1 May 1852, with 25 men signing up. Over the next 13 years the club moved around at a great pace, finding homes in Garville Avenue, Lord Palmerston's estate and South Circular Road before finding a permanent base at the end of Observatory Lane in Rathmines. The guiding light of Leinster during these early days was George Frith Barry, the captain of Ireland and a substantial figure in cricket over the next 30 years. A native of Buttevant, where his family were landowners, Barry was spotted as a youth by the Earl of Carlisle who was on the lookout for Irish cricketers to join his Vice-Regal XI. Carlisle secured a top job in

Sir Timothy O'Brien: captained Ireland and England.

Dublin Castle for Barry, where he remained for the rest of his days.

Leinster hosted the first visit to Ireland of the All England XI in 1860 on their field in Lord Palmerston's demesne. This strong side, which included stars of the day such as Julius Caesar, Tom Hayward, Richard Daft and George Parr, were too strong for the 22 Irishmen, who included five from the host club. After moving down to Rathmines Leinster again hosted the Irish 22 in their game against the United South of England XI in 1865 and several more games against the touring elevens up to 1869 when Ireland played their last 'odds' game and last against such professional sides.

The club tried their hand at promoting big games themselves and brought W.G. Grace to Ireland for the first time in 1873 for a game against 22 of Leinster. The Englishmen escaped with a draw but the following season W.G. was in sparkling form, scoring 153 while his brother GF made 103 in a total of 431. The game was a financial disaster due to a clash with the Kingstown Regatta and the club promoted no more such fixtures. The ground did, however, have distinguished visitors in December 1875 when the first rugby international, against England, took place there – much to the chagrin of their rivals at Lansdowne Road.

The schools scene was rapidly developing with Clongowes acquiring a Protestant rival at St Columba's College, where the game had been played shortly after its foundation in Stackallen, County Meath in 1843. The school moved to its current home Whitechurch, County Dublin six years later, the compact cricket field being carved out of the steep slope of Kilmashogue Hill where the game is still played today in a spectacular setting overlooking the city. A tradition of hiring masters out of Oxford and Cambridge helped the development of the game there and the school was a powerful nursery for some of Ireland's greatest cricketers of the Victorian era.

Above left: Newspaper advertisement for the 1860 game at Ormeau.

Above right: Australians v XVIII men of NICC, Ormeau, June 1880.

The only twentieth century Test cricketer to play for an Irish school, Charles 'Father' Marriott, entered St Columba's in 1912 after spending three years at the Royal School Armagh having moved from his native Lancashire for health reasons. He made quite an impact, knocking over a school record 85 wickets in 1913, including 9-3 against St Andrew's and 11-70 against High School in the Leinster senior cup final. C.S. Marriott's sojourn in the Dublin Mountains shaped his cricket in one important respect. Many years later he wrote about seeing the great Sydney Barnes bamboozle the 1912 Australians at Woodbrook.

> 'I learned more about the art of bowling in those twenty overs than I did in all the rest of my life. In the train back to Kingstown after drawing of stumps I sat in a dream, muttering to myself 'I WILL learn to do it, I WILL learn'.

Marriott, after serving in France in the Great War, made his debut for Lancashire in 1919 but because of teaching commitments only played serious cricket in the holidays. For many years he was considered the best leg-break bowler in England but played only one test for England, against West Indies in 1933 when he returned fabulous match figures of 11-96.

In 1874 Lawrence's Handbook reports that Thomas Turbett of Phoenix organised the first Irish Schools v English Schools international the previous summer – which Ireland won – but the journal was off the mark as at least five fixtures were played 20 years earlier. A game styled as Irish Schools v English Schools was played in College Park in 1855. Two future internationals (and provosts of the university), Anthony Traill and John Mahaffy were in the Irish side, but without scorecards it is hard to gauge whether these games were truly representative. One theory has it that they were between local boys who were at school in the respective countries, perhaps at half-term as the games were all played in late May. In 1857 Ireland were all out for 44 and 102, which was more than enough to beat the visitors' 36 and 27. Ireland – and the weather – got the better of the rest of the games, which carried on for another five years at least.

While the schools and clubs were advancing themselves, moves began to bring them together under the banner of regional unions. Phoenix's self-appointed role

Phoenix, 1882. Back: Rev T. Hartley, A.S. Hussey, William Hone Jnr, George Casey, W. Alexander, C.D. Barry; Front: Capt. McLaren, David Trotter, Nat Hone, F.D. Rhodes, Leland Hone.

as Marylebone-on-the-Liffey irked the Dublin clubs and was regularly challenged, particularly by Trinity. It proved impossible to agree any formal body until the Northern Cricket Union was founded in February 1884 after a meeting in No 5 Donegall Square in Belfast. The city was in the midst of a boom caused by the linen and shipbuilding industries, growing in population from 98,000 in 1880 to 350,000 in 1900, as a time when the number of people on the island was falling. One of the early aims of the NCU was to promote inter-county cricket, and the first game under their auspices was between Antrim and Down on 10-11 July. Five men from the Ulster club, four from NICC and two from Cliftonville took on a selection of four from North Down, three from Banbridge and one each from Holywood and NICC (which suggests it was county-of-origin rather than club affiliation which was the consideration for selection).

The county cricket notion died a death – strangely, among sports only the GAA uses the English-imposed county system – but the NCU's success was assured when it organised a challenge cup competition for its member clubs in 1887. Soccer was gathering adherents in the Belfast area and it was hoped the new competition would counter this. A magnificent trophy was commissioned and displayed in a Belfast shop window 'where it elicited general admiration'. The first running of the cup involved 11 sides, with North Down beating NICC at Ormeau by an innings and five runs in the final. Two members of the famous Andrews family were on the winning side. One of the great northern families, the Andrews included in their number a Stormont Prime Minister, Lord Chief Justice and two cricket internationals as well as their best-known son, Thomas, who built and died on the RMS Titanic.

With the newly-formed NCU established, moves began to form an Irish union, and in May 1884 the Freeman's Journal gave notice of a meeting, but nothing came of this attempt. Inter-union activity at club level was well-established, with North, Phoenix, Cork County and Trinity annually visiting the other unions for matches. The NCU organised inter-provincial games against the County Derry Cricket Union in June 1890, with the visitors victorious in a dismal match when they bowled the CDCU out for 24 when chasing 58 to win. The return at Ormeau ended in farce when the Derrymen walked off on the brink of defeat at 141-9 with an hour to play, claiming they had to catch the train home!

These games acted as a trial for the Ulster side in the first inter-provincial championships, played in Rathmines the following month. This was to prove an auspicious week, as it was then that moves began anew to form an Irish cricket union. The actual series, involving three two-day matches, suffered with the weather. Munster hung on for a draw with Leinster in the opening fixture, but were demolished in just one day by Ulster, for whom Willie Turner of North Down took 13-38; Ulster were set 36 to win and got it for eight wickets! Only 30 minutes play was possible on the first day of the 'final' but a sunny Saturday saw Leinster bowl out the northerners for 26 thanks to Booth and Nunn of Phoenix, and claim the first inter-provincial title.

During that week an initial meeting was held at Rathmines with Sir George Colthurst from Cork in the chair. They reconvened in Phoenix the following evening with George Barry presiding and made good progress, collecting £30 towards expenses and Barry was asked to nominate a committee. However the delicate situation was ruined one week later when the self-styled 'Leinster Branch of the Irish Cricket Union' announced its rules, assuming powers that hadn't been agreed and antagonising the NCU and Phoenix.

The row ensured that the new national organisation was charged only with arranging and organising international games, and limped along in such a role until 1924 when it was put on a more formal footing in the wake of the Treaty and the new political arrangements. The Irish Cricket Union that finally superseded it in 1933 remained firmly under the control of the delegates of the provincial unions, and it was not until 2001 that it was fully recognised as the governing body of cricket in Ireland.

It was not a harmonious passage from 1890 to the new union, and most of the rows had Phoenix at their centre. Selection for games in Dublin – and all internationals were played there – was controlled by the Leinster Branch. In 1899 the national body arranged a match at the Vice-Regal Lodge against I Zingari. Phoenix complained that they hadn't enough representation on the side – they had six! – and five of them withdrew. Phoenix seceded from the branch after this perceived slur. The English side demolished the weakened Irish side by an innings and 87 runs, with Sir Timothy O'Brien, recently retired from Middlesex, scoring 121 for the visitors. O'Brien, who captained England during the 1895-96 tour to South Africa, was to turn out several times for his native land over the next decade.

There was another row two years later when Trinity passed their invitation to host South Africa on to Phoenix. The 'premier club' organised the game for their ground but there were objections by Pembroke and Leinster who forbade their players to play. The leading northern player, Oscar Andrews, refused an invitation, saying Phoenix had no right to assume control of a representative fixture. Eventually eight Phoenix players turned out for Ireland alongside two Trinity students and one man from County Kildare, losing by five wickets.

The following winter proved decisive – Phoenix dug in, stating that they disapproved of the whole notion of an Irish union, but the intervention of Sir John Kennedy, a respected figure from County Kildare, calmed things down. His intercession between Phoenix, the other Dublin clubs, the NCU and Cork County produced a peace formula which set up the Committee for Control of Irish Representative Cricket, although the northern union was unhappy at the lack of consultation. Leinster would become an autonomous unit and cease calling itself the 'Leinster Branch'. Relations were tense for the rest of the decade, with the NCU declining to host Ireland v India and both sides pulling out of inter-provincials. When Leinster apologised for such a slight in 1909 and suggested reopening the ICU debate. NCU secretary Bob Erskine replied 'No delegates will be going south to discuss the matter. The so-called Irish Cricket Union is not formally constituted and the Northern Cricket Union will not be joining.'

The clubs in the west of Ulster had been slower to band together, but the success of the initial NCU challenge cup seemed to act as inspiration. The County Derry Cricket Union was formed in 1888 and moved quickly to organise a cup competition. Twelve sides entered: Ebrington, Limavady, Sion Mills, Donemana, Dungiven, Waterside, St Columb's Court, Ardmore, Ballymoney, Garrison, Terrydoo and Strabane. It was quite a surprise when Sion lost the semi-final to Limavady, who met Donemana in the final. A large crowd thronged the St Columba's Court ground at Lone Moor Road and saw Gault of Limavady take ten wickets as his side won a low-scoring game by 31 runs. The game made a profit of £7 12s (£7.60), even with the deduction of £1 10s (£1.50) for 'liquor at the semi-finals'.

The cup continued for six seasons before it was replaced by a league from 1894 to 1897 when competition ceased after just five teams entered. Apparently the small sides resented being beaten by the likes of Sion and Ballymoney and reverted to parochial challenge fixtures. The cup resumed in 1903 and a league was added the following season. Eventually the County Derry Cricket Union, with teams in Derry, Donegal, Antrim, Fermanagh and Tyrone realised the irrelevance of its name and re-branded itself the North-West of Ireland Cricket Union.

In the south the 1890 moves also sparked the Leinster Cricket Union into life, but

Cricket on the Mall in Armagh, 1860.

Limavady Cricket Club 1st XI
Holders for 1888 of the County Derry Challenge Cup

Back: T. McLean, R. Marshall, W.J. Moore, R. Donaghy, W. Gault
Front: G.I.K. Moriarty, St. G. MacCarthy, (Captain), J.I Allen, J. Brown (Secretary), R.J. Sherrard, J. Sherrard

Left: Limavady Cricket Club, winners of the County Derry Challenge Cup in 1888. Back row: T. McLean, R. Marshall, W.J. Moore, R. Donaghy, W. Gault, Front row: G.I.K. Moriarty, St. G. McCarthy, J.I0 Allen, J. Brown, R.J. Sherrard, J. Sherrard.

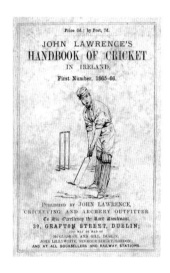

Above left: The first number of the Handbook of Cricket in Ireland, 1865-66.

Above right: Emile McMaster, born in County Down, who played only one first-class match – a test for England.

there was strong resistance to competitive cricket by the establishment clubs and a senior cup and league was not started until after the First World War, although junior clubs competed for the Intermediate Cup from 1895 (Athy, County Kildare winning the first two finals) and the schools league began in 1906. Munster and Connaught were invited to join the new national body in 1890 but did not take up the offer after Leinster jumped the gun. In 1911 Cork County affiliated and continued to represent the province until the Munster Cricket Union was belatedly formed in the 1950s. With the new structures in place, Irish cricket was well placed to welcome the new century, but there were dark clouds on the horizon – at home and abroad.

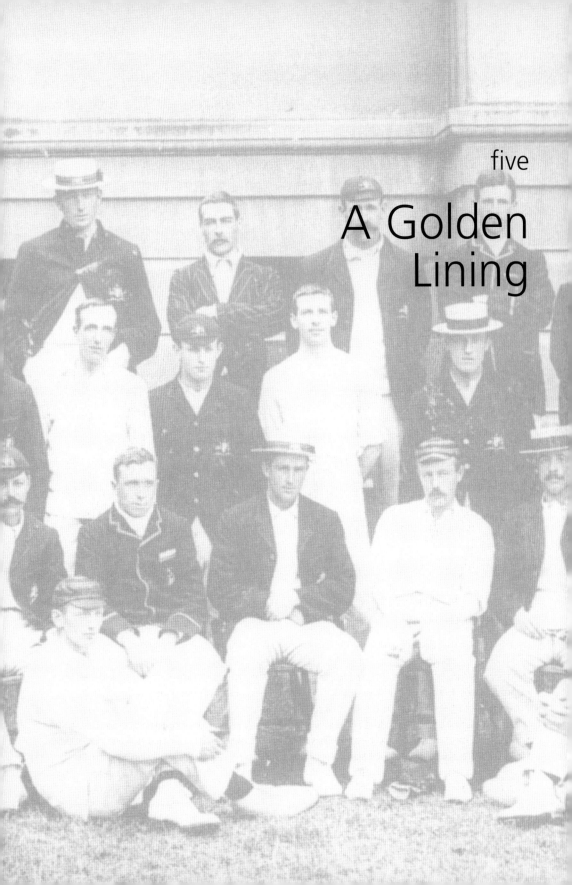

five

A Golden Lining

While cricket in Ireland began its decline, the game in England was in spectacular ascendant. The years from 1890 to the outbreak of the First World War are known as the Golden Age of Cricket, when vast crowds watched the game and players such as W.G. Grace, K.S. Ranjitsinjhi and C.B. Fry were household names. In Ireland, while the numbers playing the game were fewer, there were still quite an array of talents produced, and none greater than Lucius Gwynn.

Born in Ramelton, County Donegal in 1873, Gwynn was a star cricketer and rugby player at St Columba's before he went up to Trinity in 1890. At university he earned a raft of prizes and gold medals in Classics, as well as playing both rugby and cricket for Ireland. He was a member of the triple crown-winning rugby team in 1894, but it was in the summer game that he made most impact.

In 1895, the year known as W.G. Grace's annus mirabilis, it was actually the young Ulsterman that finished top of the English batting averages. Gwynn rattled up an unbeaten 153 against Leicestershire and 106 against Cambridge on Trinity's short tour to England. On the strength of this he was picked for the important Gentlemen v Players game at the Oval where the best of England's amateurs took on the professionals. It must have quite a morning in south London when Lucius walked out to bat with the score on 30-1. The test players George Lohmann and Tom Richardson were bowling and soon the Gents were 47-3, but Gwynn went on the attack, finishing top scorer with a brilliant 80 out of 320, finally perishing run out. He finished the season with 455 first class runs in five games – which didn't include a score of 80 for Ireland against MCC at Lord's.

The following summer, clearly having made a good impression on the powers-that-be, he again played for the Gentlemen, and was then selected to play for England against Australia at Old Trafford. Examinations in Trinity forced his withdrawal and he never again got such a chance (his place being taken by a young Indian nobleman called Ranjitsinjhi, who grew into one of the giants of the game and lived for several years in Connemara). Gwynn continued to dominate Leinster cricket, especially in 1902 when he made more than 2,000 runs. Towards the end of that summer he felt unwell and was diagnosed with tuberculosis. He travelled to Switzerland in search of clean air and a cure, but died before Christmas 1902, aged just 29.

Gwynn was part of what was arguably the strongest Irish club side ever, rivalled only by Waringstown in the 1970s and '80s. University sides are by nature cyclical, but the Trinity team of the early 1890s were blessed with talent all the way down the order. In June 1893, having won all their local fixtures, they travelled to England for a short tour. They beat Leicestershire, scoring 303 in the second innings thanks to 117 by Dan Comyn, beat Warwickshire after bowling them out for an incredible 15, and had a good draw with Essex. Oxford later visited College Park and lost by eight wickets. All-rounder Clem Johnson emigrated to South Africa at the end of the season but returned to Trinity the following summer as a member of the South African touring side. The County Kildare man played a test in 1896 alongside fellow Irishman Reggie Poore, in opposition to Dubliner Sir Timothy O'Brien. The student side enjoyed their tour to England, drawing comment in the press after walking for more than a mile through the streets of Birmingham in search of a swimming pool, clad only in their bathing costumes. That mode of dress was more scandalous to the Victorians than the student streakers that frequent College Park are in the twenty-first century.

Gwynn was one of a family of cricketers, of whom five played first-class cricket. The family tradition has been a strong one in Irish cricket, starting with the Hones, continuing with the Harrisons and on into the twenty-first century with the Joyces.

Lucius Gwynn: turned down test cap for England.

Above: Dublin University (past & present) v Australia, College Park 1905. Back row: H.H. Corley, W.W. Armstrong, J.E. Lynch, W.P. Howell, A.L. Lepper, P.A. Meldon, S.D. Lambert, Middle: Shelton (umpire), J.J. Kelly, D.R.A. Gehrs, E.R. Ensor, A. Cotter, R.M. Gwynn, A.J. Hopkins, T.A. Harvey, Dench (umpire); Seated: S.E. Gregory, C.R. Faussett, M.A. Noble, F.H. Browning, R.A. Duff, V.T. Trumper, Front row: J.T. Gwynn, P.M. Newland.

Below: Woodbrook: Sir Stanley Cochrane's private ground.

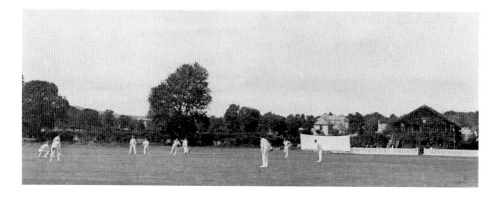

Another important cricketing clan was that of the three Meldon families, eight of whom played for Ireland and a ninth for Trinity and MCC. Among the Meldon cricketers were also internationals at tennis, soccer and hockey. A County Galway tribe, the greatest players were W.W. 'Budge' and Jack, who played for Ireland on 32 occasions from 1888 to 1910, 12 as captain. Although he was a top player of his day, perhaps the myth that it was harder to get off the Irish team than on to it started with Jack – in his last 11 games for Ireland, from 1894, he never made more than 16. He was the first man to score two centuries in a match in Ireland, 130 and 150 for Phoenix v Royal Artillery in 1909 at the age of 40. Budge emigrated to England, and then South Africa, and Irish cricket never saw him at his best. He reputedly made 100 centuries in a career which saw him play for Warwickshire and Pretoria. His greatest moment in Irish cricket was for Co Galway against Woodbrook in 1909, when he took all ten wickets for 126, a game in which Jack made 117 not out.

Woodbrook featured four professionals that day, including South African test star Bert Vogler, who also took all ten wickets. The club was a short-lived phenomenon, the plaything of Sir Stanley Cochrane, heir to the Cantrell & Cochrane soft drinks fortune. This Edwardian Abramovich was a student at Trinity for nine years from 1896, but only made the XI in 1904 – when he scored 27 runs in 24 innings. A clue to the Trinity selectors' perseverance may lie in the fact that he personally acted as guarantor for the fixture against the Australians in 1905, to the tune of £300. He also played for the university against South Africa with little success, but his taste buds had been whetted for big time cricket. In 1907 he opened a fabulous ground at his home at Woodbrook estate on the Dublin side of Bray, building a private railway station on the adjoining line to service the crowds he expected at his matches. He built an indoor school, hired several county professionals and invited touring sides and English counties to play. South Africa and Australia each visited twice, and 16 games against important sides were played at Cochrane's ground, five of which were ranked 'first-class'. Cochrane played in 13 of the big games, including one against the 1912 South Africans. He has been described as 'probably Ireland's worst first-class cricketer', a label hard to dislodge when one examines his record.

His ambitions for Woodbrook knew no bounds, and in 1912 he tried to stage a test match there. It was the summer of the triangular tournament between England, South Africa and Australia, and with one match remaining there was a chance that England and Australia would finish level. The authorities decided that in this instance a playoff would be played – but Cochrane had a contract with the Australians for the only available dates. When he was asked to give up the date, Cochrane replied that he would if the test was played in south County Dublin! As it turned out England won the final game and there was no need for any further negotiations – the Aussies came to Woodbrook to play an eleven got up by C.B. Fry and lost by eight wickets.

The Dublin clubs eventually tired of the journey out to Bray to act as cannon fodder for Cochrane's stars – Jack Hobbs and S.F. Barnes were among those hired on a match basis – and the crowds were never as great as Cochrane expected. He didn't reopen the ground in 1913 and the field later became a golf course, hosting the Irish Open in the 1970s. Cochrane's interests moved on and the indoor school became a concert hall, staging visits by the London Symphony Orchestra and Nellie Melba. Having shunned cricket for 35 years, Cochrane agreed to be first president of the Leprechauns in 1948, but died the following year. The cricket ground where Barnes' leather resounded on Hobbs' willow now echoes to the sound of titanium on surlyn but the Ladies Pavilion is obviously of cricket style and the ghost of a railway platform can still be seen from the train.

Ireland was also the venue for another footnote in cricket history when the largest partnership then recorded was made by Capt. W.C. Oates and Pte Francis Fitzgerald at the Curragh in 1895. Playing for the 1st Battallion of the Royal Munster Fusiliers against the Army Service Corps, the unbeaten stand was worth 623 with Oates, who had played for Nottinghamshire, making 313 and Fitzgerald 290. It is still the second highest stand in any form of cricket anywhere in the world. Oates' innings was the second triple hundred scored in Ireland, the previous one being made at Midleton by a visiting English sailor.

The frequent visits of I Zingari were a highlight of the Irish court social calendar. The visitors were entertained and put up at the Vice-Regal Lodge and spent much of the week attending balls and banquets. At one such dinner during the 1901 game, the Lord Lieutenant, Lord Cadogan asked Sir Timothy O'Brien to organise a tour in England for the Gentlemen of Ireland, which Cadogan agreed to underwrite. The tour took place in May 1902, and four first class games were played against London County, MCC, Oxford and Cambridge. W.G. Grace's London side were weak and Harrington and Ross took eight wickets each in a 238-run victory. Ross took 7-42 against MCC at Lord's in a rainy draw and was again in the wickets (6-92) at Oxford but Ireland were set an impossible 429 to win. Despite 167 by O'Brien, an Irish record for 70 years, a 62-run defeat ensued. The final game was won thanks to 11 wickets by Harrington.

Grace brought his side to Cork to play Ireland the following summer as part of the International Exhibition staged in the city and got into a spat with Sir George Colthurst of the host club. The Grand Old Man was out for 1 in the first over of the match but tried to bully the umpire into allowing him to stay. Colthurst marched out to the middle to remonstrate with Grace, who apologised and sheepishly followed him to the pavilion. The following season South Africa visited Cork, and they were sent packing by 93 runs. Ross was unplayable, returning figures of 17.5-6-28-9. Belfast-born, but a Phoenix player, he was a slow medium bowler and lethal on the right sort of wicket. On the strength of his excellent tour in 1902 he was selected for the Gentlemen against the Players at Lord's.

Irish selections were heavily biased towards Dublin and Cork, with few northerners winning caps, much less north-westerners. One Ulsterman who was selected far less than he might have been was Oscar Andrews, a NICC all-rounder who won eight caps from 1902-09. Starting with North Down, in 1897 against North he became the first man to score a century in the NCU cup final. At club level he was predominant for the first two decades of the century, winning nine cups and seven leagues from 1900 to 1912 after he moved to NICC. Willie Turner of North Down was never capped, despite being unrivalled in the '80s and '90s, taking a record 130 wickets in 1887. One Ulster cricketer who did gain representative honours was Emile McMaster from Gilford, County Down, who was capped by England in South Africa in 1888-89. He scored a duck on what was also his only first-class appearance.

For Ireland, infrequent fixtures against tourists were not enough, and in 1909 an annual three-day series began against Scotland that lasted for more than 90 years. As a measure of skill and progress it became the most important test each summer and was awarded first-class status by MCC. The fixture grew out of a suggestion by W.G. Grace in 1908 that a 'triple crown' competition be organised among the four nations that occupy the neighbouring islands. A regular fixture against Wales did not happen until the 1920s, and then intermittently. There was no formal championship until the 1990s when the Triple Crown one-day tournament became an annual event with Ireland, Scotland and Wales joined by a side representing the amateur game in England.

Above: Gentlemen of Ireland v South Africa, Phoenix, 1901. Back row: H. Shelton, C.G. Mitchell, Tom Ross, Blayney Hamilton, Gus Kelly, Thomas Harvey, Bill Harrington, Robin Gwynn; Seated: Lucius Gwynn, Frank Browning, Dan Comyn; Front row: Harold Denham, unknown.

Below left: Willie Pollock, leading batsman with Holywood and NICC.

Below right: Gus Kelly and Bob Lambert: Giants of the Golden Age.

The first Ireland v Scotland game to be called first-class was in 1911, when there was a high-scoring draw in Glasgow. Ireland's 409-4 declared included 149 by debutant the Hon. Henry Mulholland and 103★ by Bob Lambert. Mulholland, whose family seat was at Ballywalter Park, never played again (he was later speaker of the Stormont House of Commons) but Lambert was one of Ireland's greatest and longest-serving players.

R.H. Lambert scored 101 centuries in all cricket, and played 52 times for Ireland from 1893 to 1930, scoring almost 2,000 runs. He made 115 v Mr WH Laverton's XI in his debut season at the age of 19 – and is still the youngest Irish centurion. He was a wonderful player to watch, a dashing stylist always looking to score and possessing a powerful straight drive and effective hook. He was without parallel in club cricket, scoring mountains of runs on the good pitches at Rathmines. In 1895 he made 248★ in just over two hours against Fitzwilliam, later taking 8-23; and was only the second man to pass 2,000 runs in a season. He did the double of 1,000 runs and 100 wickets for 19 consecutive seasons and three times did the 2,000/200 double. He was highly rated by Grace, who invited him to play for London County against Lancashire, and he top scored with 49★. W.G. was asked by a journalist if Lambert would have been an even greater cricketer had he played regularly in England, to which he replied 'How do you improve on perfection?'

In the first season after the war he finished with an average of 217 to win the first Marchant Cup. He was recalled by Ireland in 1930 and took 4-102 in his last game, which began the day after his 56th birthday! His brother, Sep, and two of his sons, Ham and Drummond, also played for Ireland; Drummond's international career ended before his father's did. In July 1914 Lambert scored 68 in Rathmines as Ireland narrowly lost to Scotland, but the drums were already starting to beat in Europe after the assassination of the Austrian archduke two weeks before. Ireland, and Irish cricket, were about to enter one of the darkest periods of its history.

six

All Changed, Utterly

The outbreak of the First World War was a pivotal moment in Irish history. Ten years after the death of the old Avondale cricketer Parnell in 1891, his divided party finally reunited under the old Clongowes cricketer, John Redmond. The Irish party finally secured the passage of the Home Rule Act in 1913 but there was strong and armed resistance in the northern counties. The war put Home Rule and imminent civil war on hold and hundreds of thousands of Irishmen, north and south, volunteered for action.

Redmond supported the war effort and enlisted Sir Tim O'Brien to help drill his Irish Volunteers. Both men suffered grievous loss on the battlefields – O'Brien's eldest son, also Timothy, died on the Somme in 1916, while Redmond's brother and fellow MP Willie was killed in Flanders in 1917. At least 35,000 Irishmen died in action, among them many cricketers. An honours board was erected at Ormeau to the 253 members of the North of Ireland cricket and rugby clubs who served in the war, listing the sixty men who died. The board was extended after the Second World War, when another 28 gave their lives. Sixty-one North Down members fought, and 16 never came home.

Four of those who died from all the Irish clubs had represented their country: In 1915 James Ryan of Northamptonshire was killed at Loos and Henry Etlinger of Phoenix and Trinity was also killed in action. In 1918 Arthur Bateman, an Armagh man who played for Trinity, was listed 'missing in action' in France.

The best-remembered Ireland cricketer to die in the war, however, was a Galway man who was shot down by 'friendly fire' over Italy in January 1918, aged 37. Robert Gregory crossed paths with many of the most remarkable people of his time as the son of Lady Augusta Gregory, founder of the Abbey Theatre and instigator of the Irish Literary Revival. Gregory grew up at Coole Park near Gort, which was quite a centre for literary and artistic endeavour and Robert was a painter of some repute. W.G. Grace visited for the fishing and shooting, while W.B. Yeats, J.M. Synge and Augustus John were frequent guests. Cricket was played on the estate – George Bernard Shaw insisted that a member of staff chase the ball for him when he fielded – and master Robert became a notable player. He joined Phoenix and won selection for Ireland against Scotland at Rathmines in 1912. It turned into one of the most remarkable debuts, and still sits high on the table of best bowling performances for Ireland.

The Scots won the toss and opted to bat, and had reached 29 without loss when George Meldon tossed the ball to Gregory. Bowling medium-paced leg-breaks and cutters, he carved swathes through the batting, finishing with figures of 23-2-80-8 as the visitors collapsed to 147. Ireland replied with 98 and when the Scots were routed for 83 (Gregory 1-12) the target was set at 133. Ireland fell four runs short, with Gregory dismissed for his second duck of the match, a disappointing end to a fabulous debut. Ireland played just two more games before the war and Gregory wasn't selected for either.

Yeats wrote four powerful poems about Robert, including 'An Irish Airman Foresees His Death', the opening lines of which summed up the war for many Irishmen:

'I know that I shall meet my fate
Somewhere among the clouds above,
Those that I fight I do not hate
Those that I guard I do not love.'

Thousands of cricketing sons of Ulster marched towards the Somme with the 36th Ulster Division and many of them never took guard again. Major Holt Waring, patron of Waringstown, died leading his men at Nemal Hill in 1918. His brother Ruric had been killed three years earlier. George 'Skipper' Gaffikin, a much-loved member of Holywood

Capt of Coole to Lough Cutra Umpire - What!
Out! Did you ever see a cricket match before?
You ___!! (with hauteur) No, I am a gentleman.

Above: Coole Park v Lough Cultra, a cartoon by Robert Gregory.

Right: Robert Gregory (centre) playing for Co Galway in 1909, alongside Budge Meldon and J.J. Carroll. In front are Philip and George Meldon.

for whom he played in three cup finals, perished at the Somme, where Jack Pollock, brother of the NICC legend Willie and himself a member of the 1912 cup winning team, also fell.

All competitive cricket was cancelled in the provinces for the duration, but schools inter-provincials and other fixtures continued on a friendly basis. In Cork the game continued much as before, with many military sides spending their leave playing on the Mardyke. In one such fixture in 1917, a Corporal Hallows made 189 for Cork County against the Military of Ireland. Charlie Hallows (who later coached Belvedere College) had a long career with Lancashire and played two tests for England. Trinity College provided 3,500 students and graduates for the colours, and hundreds died, including four members of the 1913 first XI and 17 cricketers in all. College Park closed to sport and became a giant vegetable patch, as did several other grounds such as Merrion.

The old Fenian maxim that 'England's difficulty is Ireland's opportunity' was seen again with the Easter Rising in 1916. The guns for the rebellion arrived in the Howth Gun Running of 1914, and again a cricketer had a major hand in history. George Berkeley, a public-school educated descendant of the philosopher Bishop Berkeley, and British army officer in the Boer and Great wars, was a very unlikely Home Ruler. A friend of Eoin McNeill, founder of the Irish volunteers (and grandfather of staunch anti-Republican Justice Minister Michael McDowell), Berkeley became convinced that physical force was required to further the Home Rule cause and agreed to fund most of the £1,500 to finance the Howth Gun Running.

Berkeley was a slow left-arm bowler who had some excellent returns for Oxford University and played twice for Ireland in the 1890s, taking 7-20 on debut. He had another brush with history in 1919 when, as a lawyer, he helped set the reparations that defeated Germany had to pay. This is cited as a major factor in the rise of Nazism so it can be argued that the Dublin-born cricketer had a pivotal role in twentieth century history at home and abroad.

Berkeley's actions at Howth inadvertently cost the life of one those he played alongside on his Ireland debut. Frank Browning, a cousin of the Hones, was a wicketkeeper/batsman and the first man to pass 1,000 runs for Ireland. A short-armed right-hander, he saved his best performances for top opposition, whether playing for Trinity or Ireland. He recorded fifties against Warwickshire, the United South of England, Cambridge, Essex and two against the 1905 Australians. Against those last two opponents he faced Charles Kortright and Tibby Cotter, names high on the list of the fastest bowlers of all time.

Browning captained Ireland 12 times and was President of what became the ICU when the Phoenix spat over the 1899 I Zingari match flared up. He resigned in support of his club but completed a unique double when he was made IRFU president in 1912. At Lansdowne Road Browning formed and marshalled a division of the Irish Volunteer Defence Force, a home guard-style body of men past military age. They drilled with empty rifles and wore an armband with 'GR' standing for 'Georgius Rex' or King George. With typical wit, they were labelled the Gorgeous Wrecks by Dubliners. On Easter Monday 1916, the GRs were returning from manoeuvres in Kingstown when news came of the seizure of the GPO by rebels. The uniformed, but unarmed, party marched towards the city but came under fire on the corner of Northumberland Road and Haddington Road. Fourteen of the veterans fell, five fatally wounded. Browning died shortly afterwards in Beggars Bush barracks, slain by a bullet paid for by a man off whose bowling he made his first stumping for Ireland.

The 1916 Rising led to an upsurge in nationalism which was reflected in Sinn Fein

Above left: George Berkeley: slow left-armer and gun-runner.

Above right: Holt Waring: died of wounds, April 1918.

replacing Redmond's party as the voice of Irish republicanism in 1918. In January 1919 the war of independence began; it was probably unwise to schedule a fixture between the Military of Ireland and Gentlemen of Ireland for the city centre College Park in June that year. Just after 5.30p.m. on a warm, sunny day, two gunmen cycled up Nassau Street and parked their bicycles at the kerb where dozens of spectators were watching play through the railings. The gunmen fired seven shots with revolvers through the fence, presumably at the soldier cricketers who were fielding. Newspaper reports suggested that the crowd thought some of the players had been hit but the soldiers had merely dived prone. The gunmen remounted their bikes and cycled away, but their murderous salvo caught 20-year-old Kathleen Wright in the back, and the arts student died later in hospital. After about 15 minutes play resumed but shortly afterwards the Provost came onto the ground and the game was abandoned for the day.

The 'time of the Breaking of Nations' proved devastating to one important facet of Irish cricket. The landed gentry, who had provided grounds and patronage for dozens of clubs outside the city, were decimated by the European war and the bloodshed that followed in Ireland. Many of the great houses were torched by republicans, leading to mass exodus by a class already reeling from huge losses of its menfolk in the war. Castle Bernard in Bandon, a regular stop on I Zingari tours, was burnt down and the Earl kidnapped. Sir Timothy O'Brien's Lohort Castle, also in County Cork, was burned down in the black and tan war, apparently because the IRA believed it was occupied by the military. It was an ironic blow for the Home Ruler O'Brien, who was no member

Lord Dunsany: patron of cricket and poetry.

of the ascendancy. His baronetcy was inherited from his grandfather, a Catholic Dublin publican and Liberal MP who happened to be Lord Mayor of Dublin when Queen Victoria visited in 1849.

At Dunsany, near Trim in County Meath, where cricket had been played for many years under the benevolent eye of the Plunkett family, the incumbent lord was a noted writer and patron of the poet Francis Ledwidge. Dunsany recalled the summer of 1914 as the most memorable summer of all he spent in Meath:

> 'I played a little more cricket at Dunsany, and elsewhere with the Shulers, and Ledwidge continued to send me new poems, and summer shone on a world that was all at peace; but the sands of that world were running out and were almost gone.'

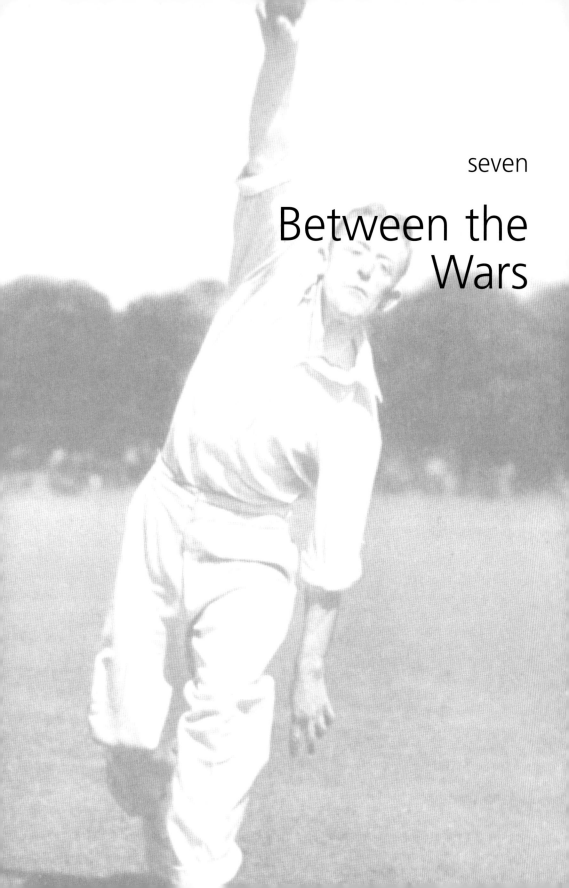

seven

Between the Wars

The butchery on the battlefields was still fresh in the memory when cricket resumed after the war. The NCU officially reformed on 3 March 1919 and its first act was to move a vote of sympathy to those who had made 'the supreme sacrifice'. Play resumed in the provinces in 1919, when the LCU finally accepted competitive cricket with the inauguration of the Leinster Senior League. The opening campaign featured nine clubs, Phoenix, Leinster, Pembroke, Trinity, Railway Union, Civil Service, UCD, County Kildare, and the Royal Hibernian Military School, but the last three were to drop out of senior – or disappear completely – over the next decade. Civil Service were relegated a number of times before leaving the senior league in 1944.

The departure of the apparatus of British rule was a blow to the membership of several clubs. The military sides packed up, obviously, but hundreds of civil servants and members of the vice-regal court also left the city and its clubs. The league was dominated in the '20s by the Leinster side led by Bob Lambert, and by a Phoenix side that included two top-class English recruits. Leslie Kidd was a Cambridge blue pre-war and joined Guinness in Dublin. His all-round skills were still highly rated in England and he played for Middlesex throughout the decade on his summer holidays. Jack Crawfurd was an Oxford blue and had played for Ireland since 1907.

Leinster's leading all rounder was Eddie Ingram, who played much of his cricket in London – including some games with Middlesex – where he worked for several years. A former schoolmate of Jimmy Boucher, he too was capped in his teens. Ingram was prolific in club cricket, with one spectacular run in 1933 – 103★, 100★, 64, 213, 86 and 65 – winning him the batting and all-rounder trophies. In 1935 team-mate Frank Connell had a similar run of three hundreds in four games as Leinster won the league for the eighth year in succession. They also won two more before the war.

Ulster historian Clarence Hiles hails the inter-war period as the halcyon days of the NCU, with big crowds for games and several star players. The era was dominated by North Down, who won 11 cups and eight leagues. The Comber side was packed with star players such as Willie Andrews – who captained the club for 39 consecutive seasons – D.R. Taylor, Albert Anderson, Jack Dearden, David McKibbin, Fred McMurray, Willie Millar, Victor Metcalfe, Henry Morgan and the Macdonald brothers James and Tom. Every one of the above played for Ireland in a time when the Irish selectors were criticised for an anti-Ulster bias.

James Macdonald is regarded as the finest all-rounder to come from the NCU. A stylish batsman and opening bowler, he made his debut for Ireland as a teenager in 1926, when he scored 95, and went on to win 29 caps. He scored one century, against MCC, and his bowling won much praise, most notably from the 1938 Australians, when the journalist and former Test player A.A. Mailey said it was the best left-arm spin he had seen all season. It was for North Down that Macdonald was seen at his greatest, however. He played in 13 cup finals from 1924 to the outbreak of war, winning nine. He set a cup record 197 against CPA in 1930, and a cup final record of 159★ against Cliftonville in 1935, completing the rare double of 1,000 runs and 100 wickets on several occasions in the decade. He served with the Royal Artillery in the war but poor health thereafter meant he didn't resume cricket.

The North-West also enjoyed a boom period between the wars. Billy Platt's history of the period is titled: 'The Greatest Years in North-West Cricket 1919-41' and he asserts that the standard of play was at its highest in the 1930s. Sion Mills were a powerful side throughout the period and had strong rivals in City of Derry in the '20s and Strabane in the '30s. There were several excellent players at the time, none better than the first

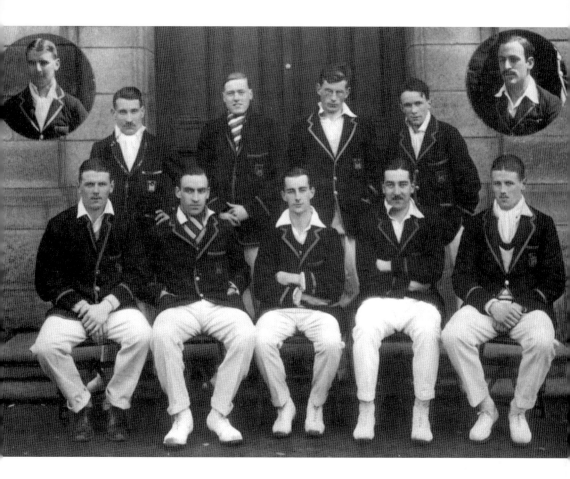

Dublin University colours XI, 1925, with a future Nobel literature laureate in the back row, third from the left. Back row: Burry McMahon, George McVeagh, Samuel Beckett, Reggie Peacocke, Front: Acheson Kelly, Mark Sugden, Jim Pigot, Arthur Robinson, Gus Kelly Jnr, Insets: Thomas Carey and Charlie McCausland.

north-westerner to play for Ulster – and for Ireland – Andy McFarlane, and English-born Donald Shearer. McFarlane was a talented all-rounder whose senior career started late because of the Great War. He was 20 when he made his debut for Sion, but started with a bang taking 8-13 including a hat-trick against City of Derry. Shearer remembered him years later: 'Andy's bat always appeared broad, just as Hammond's did and Cowdrey's too; he saw the ball so soon in its flight that although he was not noticeably quick on his feet, he was always in a position to play the correct stroke, and he had plenty of those.' McFarlane's broad bat smashed thousands of runs in the North-West, including 22 senior hundreds. He was picked far too late by Ireland – he was 38 – and never shone with a shamrock on his sweater. Shearer had a better Ireland career, 1,300 runs in 32 matches, including becoming the first batsman to score a hundred for Ireland at Lord's, in 1951, when he was 42. He was also a top soccer player, scoring 78 goals in one season for Derry City, including three hat-tricks, and playing for the Irish League in two wins over

Jimmy Boucher: topped English bowling averages on three occasions.

the English League. He also played soccer for Great Britain in the 1936 Olympic Games. Ireland had resumed internationals in 1920 with a visit to Edinburgh, when the side included only Bob Lambert and Basil Ward of that which played the last game six years before. Lambert picked up where he left off with 67 and 6-67 but a raw side – there were eight new caps, mostly students – and Scotland won by nine wickets. One of the Trinity freshmen was Herbert Rollins, still in his teens. Rollins scored more than 1,000 runs that season and started the 1921 campaign with 133 against UCD and 94 against Pembroke. Within six weeks he was dead, a victim to tuberculosis, and Irish cricket had lost a potential legend.

The LCU had proposed formalising the Irish union in 1920 but were rebuffed by the NCU as they felt 'the time is inappropriate', a reasonable enough reply given the state of near-anarchy in much of the country. There were further attempts in 1921 and 1922 but Ulster said 'No' on each occasion. In 1923 the NCU agreed that there should be discussions about a union – although the North-West were not involved in the negotiations – and the following year the union was formed, run by four representatives from Ulster, four from Leinster and two from Munster. Its powers were strictly limited by the unions and it was renamed as the Irish Cricket Union in 1933.

Above left: Eddie Ingram: Dubliner who played for Middlesex.

Above right: Jack Crawfurd: English recruit for Phoenix.

Over the next four years the only fixtures were annual games with Scotland and, for the first time, Wales. In 1922, after 12 years out of the Ireland team, William Pollock marked his return with 144 against Scotland. MCC fixtures resumed but the first visit of a touring side post-war came in 1923 when the West Indies arrived for fixtures against Trinity (who they beat by eight wickets) and a NCU XI (who hung on for a draw). The northern unions had much cause to complain about their treatment at the hands of the IRCCC. Opportunities were few for their players and their grounds were shunned when fixtures were being handed out. It wasn't until 1924 that an Ireland team played a home game outside Dublin or Cork, when Wales visited Ormeau. It was Ireland's one hundred and eleventh international and, in an obvious attempt to redress the balance, seven Ulster players were selected.

The next West Indians to tour, four years later, featured in one of the greatest games ever seen in Ireland. While not as revered as the 1969 win, Ireland's performance against a team shortly to make its test debut – and thus far unbeaten in 13 matches in England – resulted in a stunning victory. The three-day game started on 4 June in College Park, with the tourists missing just two leading players and Ireland without James Macdonald who was doing exams at Queen's and the unavailable Leslie Kidd. Winning the toss, Ireland were rattled early by the pacy Griffith and Small, losing Louis Bookman to the second ball of the day, but captain Jim Ganly and Tom Jameson made forties and recovered somewhat to 173 all out by mid afternoon. The West Indies fared no better and were 100 for six at the close and were dismissed for 142 on the second morning.

Above left: Andy McFarlane: few opportunities.

Above right: James Macdonald: finest Northern all-rounder.

Below: Sion Mills, winners of the 1938 North-West Senior League.

The hesitant batting that both sides had shown continued into Ireland's second innings and although Bookman atoned with 31, and Ganly made the same score, Ireland were on 92 when George McVeagh came to the crease at the fall of the sixth wicket.

A 21-year-old student at Trinity, the Meathman had been playing for Ireland for two seasons but was yet to pass 50. The left-hander had made buckets of runs for the college, including 67 against a Northants side and four centuries the previous season, three unbeaten in succession, when Trinity had won the league. With Leinster all-rounder Jacko Heaslip making 44, they saw the score to 173-7. Debutant Patrick Thornton, the son of a South African test player who himself would play there for Border, joined his fellow student in the attack.

The pair added 103 in the next 90 minutes before Thornton was out for 37 just before the close, when McVeagh was 85 not out. The ninth wicket fell immediately on the final day but another Trinity team-mate, Australian-born Tom Dixon, held on to ensure McVeagh posted an incredible century. Ganly, writing about the match 50 years later, said he would never forget the excitement when a cover drive just reached the rope under the scoreboard to raise the hundred. McVeagh had batted three-and-a-half hours for his unbeaten 102, including ten fours. Set a stiff 352 to win, the West Indies set about it purposefully, making 117 before the first wicket fell, with McVeagh diving to hold a high one-handed catch on the leg-side boundary to dismiss Clifford Roach for 71. The tourists were still well-placed on 213-2 before Seymour, Dixon and Jameson – and four catches by the unstoppable McVeagh – dismissed them for 291, sixty runs short with just four minutes left.

McVeagh was quite an all-round sportsman, captaining Ireland at cricket and tennis and also winning caps at hockey and squash. It was a great era for all-round sportsmen, a phenomenon that has all but died out. Ganly was a rugby and tennis international, while Lithuanian-born Bookman was capped at soccer. Other cricket internationals of the period who played for Ireland at other sports include James Macdonald and Jack Bowden (hockey), John Harris and Billy McCleery (soccer), Arthur Douglas, Bob Alexander, Finlay Jackson, Mark Sugden, George Morgan, David Taylor, Ham Lambert and Bobby Barnes (rugby), Cecil Pemberton (table-tennis) and Sir Basil Goulding (squash). NICC batsman Gilbert Cook even played rugby for England!

The next visitors were the Catamarans, an Indian side got up by the Nawab of Pataudi, a nobleman who played for England before India played tests. Ireland won a low-scoring game by 76 runs, but Pataudi broke the College Park ground record with 233 the same week. Presumably the groundsman kept the best wicket for the student XI. The international was most notable as the debut of arguably the greatest bowler to play for Ireland, James Chrysostom Boucher.

In an international career that carried on till 1954, Jimmy took 307 wickets in 60 games. Bowling brisk off-spin, he imparted a savage tweak on the ball with his fingers, described by long-serving ICU secretary Derek Scott as resembling 'a bunch of bananas'. His late-dipping deliveries deceived countless top batsmen and he picked up most wickets in the region of short-leg. Boucher made his senior debut at 14 for Civil Service in 1925, before moving to neighbouring Phoenix. An attacking bowler, his record of 1,309 wickets (at an average of 11.48) in Leinster competition is unlikely to be equalled, as is the fact that he three times topped the English first-class averages, in 1931, 1937 and 1948. He was a more than useful batsman – 'the best No 8 in the world' he used to say – and topped the LCU averages in 1939. Most knowledgeable observers say he would have had a long and distinguished career with a county, and might even have played test cricket. When his long career ended with a back complaint in 1954, he took on the job as ICU Hon Secretary, a post he filled for two decades and his high standing in England led to increased links and opportunities for Irish cricket.

Ireland were beaten by ten wickets by the 1936 Indians, but the fixture against the New Zealanders the following summer was one of the most extraordinary ever seen at Rathmines. Only 219 runs were scored on the first day, but as 32 wickets fell – 20 of them Irish, the whole match was over in one day. Ireland made 79 all out before Boucher routed the Kiwis for 64, taking 12-5-13-7. If Ireland ever scented victory, it was a short-lived dream, as they were themselves skittled for just 30 in 18.2 overs, with Jack Cowie finishing with 8-5-3-6 and the visitors lost two wickets making 46. The visitors agreed to play a two-day match which they won by an innings and 52 runs.

Rugby international Ham Lambert, son of Bob, made a hundred against Sir Julian Cahn's XI at Rathmines the following summer, but the highlight that year was the September visit of the Australians to Belfast and Dublin. The tourists travelled without the injured Don Bradman, the batting giant of that and any other era, and thus 'the Don' failed to have a game against Ireland on his otherwise immaculate CV. At Ormeau, the Australians made 145 off 62 overs as James Macdonald (16-6-24-5) and Ingram (22-7-46-4) made hay, but the total was more than enough. Bill O'Reilly, one of the greatest spinners of all time, was unplayable, returning figures of 9-6-7-3 while fellow leggie Frank Ward took 5-22 and Ireland were all out for 84, with only Tom Macdonald (28) and Ingram making double figures.

The following day, a two-day game commenced in College Park, with a huge crowd thronging the centre-city venue. Ireland made two changes, bringing in Boucher, but the Phoenix man was unfit and had a poor game. Ireland were dismissed for 100, with Mickey Williams of Pembroke top-scoring with 26 and O'Reilly again dominant with 7-5-7-3. The tourists rattled up 239 thanks to fifties by Stan McCabe, Cyril Badcock and No.10 Sid Barnes. 'Chicken' Ingram was in fine form, having McCabe stumped. At one stage after tea he had 5-18 off seven overs.

For the first ball of the second day Ingram was on a hat-trick, but he narrowly missed out on the feat and finished with 31.4-8-83-7. Hat-tricks have proved elusive for Irish bowlers, with only one ever recorded, by T.H. Hanna of NICC on his debut in 1877, against I Zingari. Hanna was a fast underarm bowler, clean bowling 118 of his 124 wickets that year.

The Australians, in their last game of a marathon tour, were clearly in demob mood and opened the bowling with reserve slow left-armer Ted White, who took 3-16, but it was again O'Reilly who vanquished the land of his ancestors with 5-39 as Ireland collapsed to 106, despite 56 in almost three hours by Donald Shearer.

The late summer of 1939 was notably warm, but there were storm clouds gathering elsewhere in Europe. Ireland finished the summer with a high-scoring game at Cahn's seat in Nottingham. Tom Macdonald marked his last game for Ireland – though he wasn't to know that – with a century as his brother James made 95. While the coming world war would not match its predecessor for blood shed by Irishmen, or Irish cricketers, it would still put a halt to international play for six long summers.

E.D.R. Shearer: first to score century for Ireland at Lord's.

Ireland v Australia, College Park, 1938. Back row: Leach (scorer), F.A. Ward, C.W. Mellon, W.J. O'Reilly, C.W. Billingsley, E.S. White, N.H. Lambert, A.L. Hassett, L.G. Watson; Middle: Brockway (umpire), W. Ferguson (scorer), E.N. Larmour, M.B. Williams, S. Barnes, T.J. Macdonald, C.W. Walker, E.A. Ingram, L. O'B Fleetwood-Smith, C.R. Cuffe, E.D.R. Shearer, Fitzsimons (umpire); Front row: W.A. Brown, J.C. Boucher, B.A. Barnett, S.J. McCabe, W.H. Jeanes, Capt. D.C. Lindsay, J. Macdonald, M.W. Waite, C.L. Badcock, J.A. Fingleton, A.E. Bex (ICU Secretary).

eight

Distinguished
Guests

The Second World War had much less impact on cricket in Ireland than the previous war. The Irish Free State remained neutral, and competitions were played as usual, but shortage of fuel meant clubs were generally confined to their local areas and several club tours to rural parts died out. Plenty of Irishmen signed up to fight – more did so from the neutral south than the north – but the wholesale slaughter of the Great War was not replicated, among the military at least.

In the northern area, league and cup competition was still played, but the winning teams were awarded sets of stumps instead of trophies. In 1940 Queen's University won the cup for the only time in its history. Many regiments trained in the North and several top players played games against local sides. Among those that turned out were England test stars Denis Compton and George Pope and Australia's Keith Miller. Strabane CC took full advantage and were able to field two players who played for Yorkshire and England: spinner Hedley Verity – who died in the Allied invasion of Italy – and batsman Norman Yardley. The pair inspired Strabane to a league and cup double in 1941, their first since 1910. When Verity was asked about Ulster wickets, he replied 'They're grand. They know what a good turn means.'

The test stars served with the Green Howards regiment, and would have fancied their chances of defeating a North-West XI in a charity match at Omagh in September 1941. Verity was in sparkling form, taking 8-55 as the locals were routed for 112. Pat Kelly of Sion Mills knocked over the first four wickets, including Verity (18) and Yardley (0) before club mate Hughie Donaghey demolished the tail with figures of 4-0-9-4 as the Green Howards were all out for 91. The North-West did away with competitions from 1940-42, but the competitive nature of cricket in the region meant that 'The Friendly League' was not popular and league and cups began again in 1943.

The south was not spared wartime pain. At 2a.m. on the morning of 31 May 1941, four bombs were dropped on Dublin by a German plane, with one landing on North Strand killing 38 people and another in Terenure killing three. The one that caused least damage fell in the Phoenix Park between the Dog Pond and the eastern boundary of Phoenix CC. Most of the pavilion windows were shattered and some debris went through the roof, but no-one was injured. The pitch was littered with earth and stones, some deeply embedded, which meant the game against YMCA that afternoon had to be called off. A shortage of materials meant the clubhouse remained without windowpanes for months. The German government made amends after the war, forwarding a cheque for £219.

The British ambassador Sir John Maffey organised several fixtures between his XI and Dublin clubs and was visited at a game in College Park by Taoiseach Eamon De Valera, who had a short stroll down Kildare Street from the Dail. Lapping the boundary with Maffey, 'Dev' picked up a bat and played a few practice shots, perhaps remembering his days in Blackrock College before playing rugby and cricket became a liability for a Sinn Fein/Fianna Fail politician. He was soon awakened from his sport by that very fear, as a press photographer moved into position to take a picture. De Valera tossed the bat away rapidly, thus avoiding stern admonition in the editorials of the Irish Press and a life ban from the Croke Park VIP box.

The first wartime champions in Dublin were Merrion, who in 1940 became the first club to complete the league/cup double. It was a remarkable feat for a club that was still playing intermediate cricket 15 years before. The double was the culmination of rapid progress since winning the intermediate league in 1923, 1924 and 1925. The club also had to recover in 1930 from the first of three devastating floods in the twentieth century of the River Dodder, which flows past the ground. The arrival of a group of

The Phoenix pavilion in 1941, with windows and slates broken by a stray German bomb.

talented cricketers transformed the club: Roly Shortt, Cecil Little and Alan O'Donnell started playing in the 1920s and were followed into the XI by Simon Curley and Paddy Waldron. It was a strong bowling and fielding performance that saw Merrion through the 1940 season unbeaten. Curley scored 112* against YMCA and was joined in the top five of the provincial averages by Kevin Dempsey, but it was the bowling of Shortt (40 wickets at 10.4) and Chris Mara (46 at 12.13) that was crucial. Mara won the all-rounders trophy to cap a remarkable season.

Representative cricket was slow resuming after the war, and Ireland played just one match in 1946, when they beat Scotland by eight wickets in Greenock. Boucher picked up where he left off with 7-75, while Armagh vicar Rev Bobby Barnes took 4-18, but the highlight was 140* by Frank Quinn of Phoenix, one of a well-named family, as the five brothers played for Phoenix, including four who played for Ireland.

The 1947 South Africans visited for three games, with off-spinner Athol Rowan taking a remarkable 9-39 in a rain-affected draw in Trinity. The next day at Ormeau

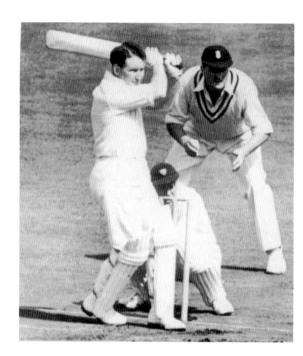

Above left: Noel Mahony: a shot to leg on his debut v MCC at Lord's in 1947.

Above right: Larry Warke pulls the ball to the boundary for Ireland.

Below left: Norman Yardley and Hedley Verity, England, Yorkshire and Strabane, 1941.

Below right: Stuart Pollock: stylish bat and brilliant fielder.

he took 10-4-10-7 and 19-10-14-5 as Ireland were routed for 32 and 61 and lost by an innings and 125 runs in one day. Remarkably, Ireland picked themselves up the next day and – in the absence of Rowan – won by six wickets when Boucher took 7-37 and Barnes made 57. Rowan was back four years later, and just as keen on Irish wickets and Irish batsmen, taking 3-49 and 7-23 in an eight wicket win at Ormeau. He was rested at College Park, but slow left-armer Tufty Mann did a similar job and a Roy McLean century secured an innings win for the tourists.

Ireland featured in a bizarre, rain-affected game at Margam in 1953, when Charles Kenny (4-14) and Eddie Ingram (4-33) bowled out Glamorgan for 81. Joy was short-lived as Ireland collapsed to 67 all out but Lloyd Armstrong took 4-16 before the county declared in 81-6. Stanley Bergin repeated his first innings 22 but Ireland were forced to hang on grimly for a draw at 81-9. It was also the only first-class game umpired by brothers, J.E.G. and W.E.P. (Tim) Protheroe-Beynon. The latter moved to Ireland where he became a leading mover in the formation of the Leinster Cricket Umpires Association and was the oldest man to umpire a first-class match when he stood in the three-day Ireland v Scotland game in 1977, at the age of 72.

The best schools players, who had been playing inter-provincials for half a century, began to be selected on Ireland Schools teams in 1950 when an annual fixture with The Leprechauns itinerant side was started. Schools internationals against Wales began in 1964, but the ICU refused to pay for the fixture and for several years players were expected to pay their own travel and accommodation for trips across the Irish Sea.

Frank Worrell's 1957 West Indians came for two games, with Alf Valentine and Garfield Sobers collecting a bag of wickets apiece, but many of the biggest stars that visited Ireland in the era were playing for MCC. Bob Wyatt was a regular throughout the decade, while England captains Donald Carr, Freddie Brown, Freddie Mann, Wally Hammond, Colin Cowdrey and Len Hutton all visited and drew large crowds. The decline in playing numbers that had been marked since the Great War continued in the 1950s and 1960s, and it was not until the widespread availability of BBC television in the 1970s that new players were drawn to the game.

In the late 1940s Sion Mills were arguably the strongest club in Ireland. Under the captaincy of W.F. Keery they developed great discipline, team spirit and competitiveness, and in John Flood they had the best bowler in North-West cricket for almost three decades. Young players such as Faulkner, Kelly, Gallagher, Duddy, Farrell, McFarlane and McCrea came into the team and in 1947 they entered the NCU senior cup and won it at the first attempt – and also did the North-West double. Over the next decade they were rivalled by Donemana and the pair had some epic battles, although when Donemana won the league for the first time in 1950 under the captaincy of Alex McBrine, they held onto it until 1955. Sion reached 11 cup finals in the 18 years from 1945, but only lost one of them. They also won six leagues in the same period as they introduced exciting young players such as future internationals Brendan Donaghey, Ossie Colhoun and Aubrey Finlay.

Colhoun played for Ireland for 20 years, and was the most capped player with 87 games when he retired in 1979. His record of 190 dismissals, 148 catches and 42 stumpings are each well clear of anyone else who wore the gloves for Ireland. A magnificent wicketkeeper, he had a rough baptism at the age of 20, and few predicted he would win eight caps, much less 87. But he was still there at the age of 40 after a senior career that began with Sion at the age of 13. Colhoun had a reputation as a bit of 'a character' and was an early-adopter of the art of sledging and gloveman chatter. In his

Munster versus Leinster, 1958. Back row: George Vardy, Jim Fitzgerald, Noel Cantwell, Barclay Wilson, Ian Lewis, Pat Dineen; Front: Jim Kiernan, Des Cashell, Tommy Williams, Jim Cronin, Tommy Odlum.

autobiography, Ireland captain Dermott Monteith recalled that he disguised his mistakes with aplomb – 'He once missed three chances in an over but nobody on the field except he and the bowler (me) knew anything about it'. His lightning fast hands were nothing to his repartee, although another Irish bowler, Mike Halliday, insisted that it would have been incomprehensible to opponents 'delivered as it was in a form of North-West Jive'. The highlight of Colhoun's long career came on his home ground when the West Indies were bowled out for 25 in 1969. His 87 caps was a record for a north-westerner until Peter Gillespie overtook him in 2005.

Another North-West favourite came to the fore in 1949, when he took 10-10 for Eglinton against Donemana. His club had been dismissed for 53, but Scott Huey's swing and cut accounted for all the Donemana batsmen who were out for 20. His slow left arm won him 36 caps from 1951-66, and was only the fifth to pass a century of wickets for Ireland, finishing with 112. He was also the first North-West player to captain Ireland when he did so in five games in the early '60s. He earned a footnote in cricket history as the last man to dismiss Sir Len Hutton when he had him stumped at College Park in 1960, while at 41 he still possessed enough guile to take 5-68 against the 1965 New Zealanders.

In the North the Lisburn side headed up by the exceptional all-rounder Jack Bowden and batsmen Herbie Martin and Tom McCloy won the league three years on the trot from 1950-52. At the same time Woodvale were the specialist cup side, winning three-in-a-row from 1948-50, and again in 1952 and 1954. That side, captained by Billy McCleery, included a young batsman fresh up from Trinity called Larry Warke. North dominated the second half of the decade, winning the league in 1954, 1957, 1960 and 1961.

Cregagh off-spinner Frank Fee had an extraordinary introduction to first-class cricket

Alec O'Riordan (third from left) leads out the Irish side against Australia at College Park, 1961. The rest of the side was Larry Warke, Mike Stevenson, Joe Hopkins (wkt), Stanley Bergin, Archie McQuilken, Herbie Martin, Raymond Hunter, Aubrey Finlay, Rodney Bernstein, Given Lyness.

in 1956. He played in one rained-off game against Sussex before being pitted against MCC in College Park. He marked the occasion with seven wickets in each innings and in his next first-class game, against Scotland, took 9-26– still the Irish record – and 3-34. In between he took 4-61 against the West Indies, including Frank Worrell and Gary Sobers. But, at the age of 25, his Irish career was over in 1959, losing form as his pace quickened. He took 58 wickets in 13 matches at 12.56.

Stuart Pollock had a far longer career in an Ireland sweater. First capped before the war, he won the rest of his 41 caps up to 1957. Son of eight-times capped former Irish captain, Willie, he too got to captain his country and was acclaimed by several watchers as the finest cover point Ireland ever had. Stuart enjoyed playing at Ormeau, making 89 there against Yorkshire in 1949 and 50 against the 1951 South Africans.

In Munster the first post-war season saw an important development with the inauguration of the Schools Senior Cup, won by Rockwell College from an entry of eight. The Munster senior provincial side commenced annual fixtures with Ulster in 1947, but the following year's game was notable for the chaotic travel arrangements. The distance from Cork to Belfast necessitated a full day's travel and overnight stays, so to save time and money it was decided to fly the players up. Only one eight-seater aircraft was available, meaning the side would be carried in two trips. Sadly the Dragon Rapide craft was not at all rapid, and the first group arrived less than an hour before the 11.30a.m. start. Noel Mahony kept his end up for hours, making 81, but Munster were

IRISH CRICKET UNION

IRELAND v. M.C.C.

1858   1958

CENTENARY YEAR

College Park, Dublin.   September 6, 8 and 9, 1958

ONE SHILLING

Programme for Ireland v MCC, 1958. The publication marked the centenary of the first game between the sides.

down to their last pair when the rest of the players arrived. The farce wasn't over as two four-seaters were hired to bring the remainder of the squad home at the same time as the Rapide. One of the tiny planes was forced to land in a field near Cahir in County Tipperary, when Cliff Read, with a copy of the New York Herald under his arm, hopped out and asked a local farmer – in a fake American accent – whether they had landed in England. 'No sir, this is County Tipperary in Ireland', came the reply!

Munster cricket in the '50s was lit up by some fine all-round sportsmen, including the rugby-playing Kiernan brothers Jim and Tom, and Noel Cantwell, captain of Manchester United and the Irish soccer team, who was five times capped at cricket. Cantwell top scored against the 1958 New Zealanders with 40, but was out for a duck against the West Indies at College Park the previous year, dismissed in as glamorous fashion as anyone ever has been: 'caught Worrell bowled Sobers'.

The Leinster trophies were shared around in the '50s, with nine different clubs winning at least one trophy. The outstanding sides were Leinster, who three leagues and four cups, including the double in 1953; and Pembroke, whose three leagues and two cups including doubles in 1954 and 1957. The Pembroke side was a classic mixture of experience and youth, with a top class batsman leading the way. Stanley Bergin, Bill Haughton, Ciaran O Maille and Mickey Williams got the runs, while Williams, Godfrey Graham and Ken Hope got the wickets, many of them snapped up by stumper Harry Hill, who ended his 30-year senior career with 502 victims. Hill was succeeded in 1977 by Colin Kavanagh, who claimed his 503rd victim in July 2005.

When long-serving Irish batsman Gerry Duffy was asked to name the best he had played with, singled out Bergin: 'Stan wasn't the toughest looking of men, but he never lacked courage. I saw him making a fifty for Ireland against Derbyshire at College Park against an English opening pace attack of Jackson and Gladwin. They gave him a terrible hammering, he was battered and bruised but he never flinched once.' Bergin played 53 times for Ireland, scoring an erstwhile record 2,524 runs, including two centuries. Bergin was just four years off the Irish team, and working as Evening Herald cricket correspondent, when he died suddenly aged 42.

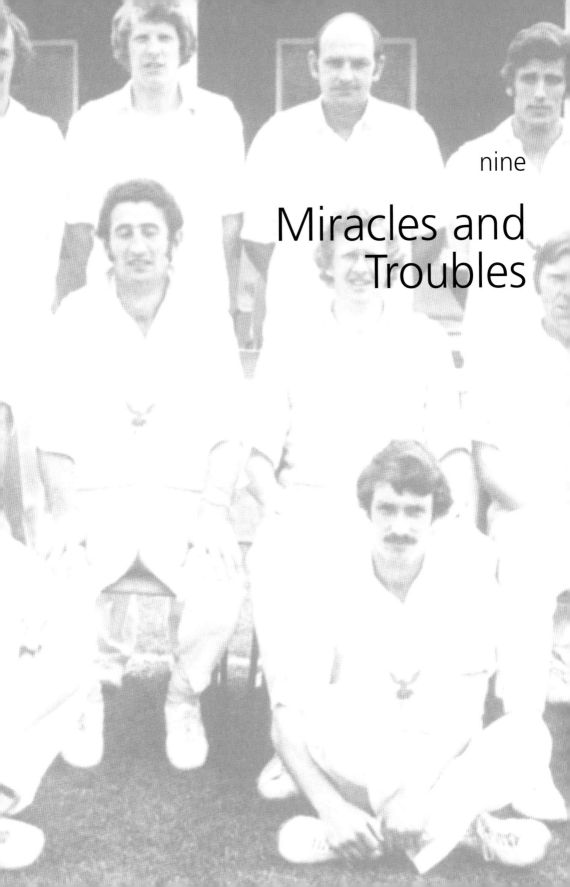

nine

Miracles and Troubles

The world was a different place in the 1960s, and Irish cricket took some giant steps forward in that decade. But the social unrest of the second half of the decade spawned a long period of armed conflict in Northern Ireland which had huge implications for the game. Heading into the new decade the ICU was successful in attracting fixtures against the counties; three such games took place in 1959 and although none was won, there was plenty to encourage with fine performances by Stanley Bergin (two sixties v Yorkshire), Scott Huey (7-84 v Lancashire) and Herbie Martin (61 v Leicestershire).

The visit of the Australians is always a highlight and Richie Benaud's 1961 team were welcome guests for two fixtures. The Belfast game started late because of rain, but when play began the Irish bowled and fielded like tigers, none more than Gerry Duffy of Leinster, who took 6-29, which included a brilliant boundary catch by Raymond Hunter to dismiss Garth McKenzie. Replying to 209, Ireland struggled against Kline and Davidson and ended the day on 72-8. Captain Alec O'Riordan (38) shepherded the tail the next morning to a total of 126. Conditions on the second day were awful – a gale force wind ripped up the press tent, a marquee and several roof tiles. The tourists deserve credit for playing on, and after Davidson entertained the crowd with a lightning 50, they declared on 155-7 to set Ireland 239 in ninety minutes. Martin made 57 as the Australian batsmen and wicketkeepers turned their arms over and the game ended with Ireland on 138-6.

Down to Trinity for another two-day game, the tourists were in full end-of-tour mode and every one of their players got a bowl at some stage. The weather was in sharp contrast to that at Ormeau and a huge crowd turned out to watch. At one stage O'Riordan had 3-11 in six overs but Brian Booth (79) and Alan Davidson (46) rattled up 63 in 35 minutes. When Davidson was out Booth and Peter Burge (60) continued the onslaught with 99 in 44 minutes. Wally Grout hit 22 off Archie McQuilken's first over but the debutant persevered and was rewarded with 4-63 as Australia made 291, O'Riordan finishing with 5-85.

Ireland's batting was a shambles, with the first seven wickets falling for 44. Bergin was top scorer with 21 but O'Riordan (16) saw Ireland to 76 all out. On the second morning the Australians cut loose, rattling up 183 runs in the first hour and a quarter. Davidson was at the heart of the assault, launching a huge straight six off Rodney Bernstein that hit the roof of the pavilion on his way to 59. Burge and Grout rattled up 39 in the last six minutes before the declaration which came at 233-6. Given Lyness was the pick of the bowlers with 4-46. Ireland had no chance of making the 449 to win, and only Hunter (50, including four successive boundaries off Kline) and O'Riordan (38*) salvaged any pride as they lost by 282 runs. Benaud was so impressed by Ireland's young captain that he presented him with his tour blazer.

If there is debate whether Jimmy Boucher or Dermott Monteith was Ireland's greatest spinner, there is little argument about O'Riordan's stature as the pre-eminent fast bowler. Schooled at Belvedere College, O'Riordan began his club career aged 14 with Clontarf before joining Old Belvedere and helping them win promotion to Senior in 1956, an astonishing development for a club only founded in 1950.

O'Riordan won the first of his 72 caps against Worcestershire aged 18, and was never dropped by Ireland. At his peak his left-arm pace was blistering and he was offered contracts by at least five English counties, but career and family kept him in Dublin. Alan Davidson told the Irish media in 1961 that had Alec been Australian he would be in the running for a test place. O'Riordan took 206 wickets for Ireland and first captained his country at the age of 20. Injuries hampered him in the 1960s but he reassumed command in 1972.

Above: Thirty years on, Dougie Goodwin and Alec O'Riordan remember the special day.

Below left: How Wisden reported the Sion Mills game.

Below right: The Daily Mirror front page the following day.

IRELAND v. WEST INDIES

At Sion Mills, Londonderry, July 2. Ireland won by nine wickets. In some ways this one-day match provided the sensation of the 1969 season. The West Indies, with six of the team who had escaped on the previous day from defeat in the Lord's Test, were skittled for 25 in this tiny Ulster town on a damp and definitely emerald green pitch. The conditions were all in favour of the bowlers, but the West Indies batsmen fell in the main to careless strokes and smart catching. Goodwin, the Irish captain, took five wickets for 6 runs and O'Riordan four for 18. Both bowled medium pace at a reasonable length and the pitch did the rest. It was not a first-class match, but Ireland's performance deserves a permanent record and therefore we give the full score.

West Indies

G. S. Camacho c Dineen b Goodwin....	1	— c Dineen b Goodwin.......	1
M. C. Carew c Hughes b O'Riordan....	0	— c Pigot b Duffy..........	25
M. L. C. Foster run out.............	2	— c Pigot b Goodwin........	0
*B. F. Butcher c Duffy b O'Riordan....	2	— c Waters b Duffy..........	50
C. H. Lloyd c Waters b Goodwin.....	1	— not out..................	0
C. L. Walcott c Anderson b O'Riordan .	6	— not out..................	0
J. N. Shepherd c Duffy b Goodwin.....	0		
†T. M. Findlay c Waters b Goodwin.....	0		
G. C. Shillingford not out.............	0		
P. Roberts c Colhoun b O'Riordan.....	0		
P. D. Blair b Goodwin..............	3		
B 1......................	1	L-b 2..................	2
	25		(4 wkts.) 78

1/1 2/1 3/3 4/6 5/6   1/1 2/2 3/73 4/78
6/8 7/12 8/12 9/12

Bowling: *First Innings*—O'Riordan 13—8—18—4; Goodwin 12.3—8—6—5. *Second Innings*—O'Riordan 6—1—21—0; Goodwin 2—1—1—2; Hughes 7—4—10—0; Duffy 12—8—2—12; Anderson 7—1—32—0.

He was a genuine all-rounder, his right-handed batting scoring 2,000 runs and three hundreds for Ireland, including a memorable 102 at Lord's in 1969 and compiling 10,700 runs at almost 35 in Leinster. He took 849 wickets at 8.88 in a senior career than spanned 34 seasons. His club won the cup three years in succession from 1964 to 1966 (following a similar run by Trinity), and O'Riordan revelled in the big occasion that was the Leinster Senior Cup final. Malahide were the opponents on each occasion of the three-in-a-row when O'Riordan took 5-36, 7-54 and 7-23. In the 1970 final against Clontarf he scored 80 and took 6-22. He topped the batting, bowling and all-rounder averages in 1965, 1975 and 1977. 'I worked hard,' he recalled in an interview with Anthony Morrissey in the 1986 Irish Cricket Annual, 'I usually took one end for the innings and when I batted mine was the wicket they were gunning for. Every summer I used to wear out a heavy pair of boots and lose a stone in weight. Bowling so many overs caused a lot of wear and tear and I began to have knee injuries in the mid '70s. After that I became a full-time batsman'.

O'Riordan was one of the heroes on the day an Ireland match made front page headlines – 2nd July 1969 – when the West Indies were bowled out for 25 at Sion Mills. There were whispers that the Windies had partied too well on Bushmills but the truth was far simpler: they had played a hard-fought draw with England at Lord's the day before and were caught cold on a wet, green wicket by two high-class bowlers. O'Riordan took 4-18 and Captain Dougie Goodwin of Malahide an astonishing 5-6 off 12.5 overs. 'They were late getting in on the plane and then had a long drive from the airport,' recalled Goodwin. 'We might have had a few, but I don't think they had time to have a drink.' The score could have been even more humiliating, as the tourists were reduced to 12-9 before the last pair more than doubled the score. West Indies manager Clyde Walcott, who played that day, devoted a chapter in his autobiography to the 'Skirmish at Sion Mills'. He agreed with Wisden in what he called 'one of the lowest points in West Indian cricket', the almanack curtly reporting that the Irish 'bowled medium pace at a reasonable length and the pitch did the rest… conditions were all in favour of the bowlers'. However, Ireland rattled past the total and on to 125 before declaring. The visitors made it to 78-4 before time ran out and under the laws for a one-day time match, Ireland won on the first innings lead. The Times headlined it 'W Indians Routed In Ireland' while the Daily Mirror put a colour photo of the bowlers on the front page under the banner 'Supermen'. Poet Morgan Dockrell, himself a good club player, commemorated the day in A Famous Victory, a stanza of which goes

> 'An Em'rald Pitch is not a Carib's friend,
> For Ireland's heroes strove like men inspired.
> While one by one the Visitors "retired";
> Their faces long, their crease-duration short.
> For Hospitality goes ill with Sport.'

With the onset of the Troubles, not every touring side was willing to risk a trip across the Irish Sea, and to increase the international programme the ICU decided to seek out opponents of similar standard and fixtures were swapped with Holland and Denmark while the series with Wales was resumed. In 1973 a tour was taken to North America, where Ireland drew with Canada and lost to the USA by 42 runs. The playing highlight of the trip was Ivan Anderson's 198 at Toronto, still the highest innings by an Irish batsman. Anderson started slowly, and after 70 minutes batting had made just 11. But once he was in he cut loose and the next three and a half hours saw him smash a further 187. He received support right down the order, with Colhoun contributing a vital 16 in

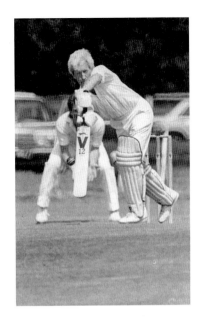

Above left: Pat Dineen batting v Holland 1971.

Above right: David Pigot, who played senior cricket in six decades.

Below left: Gerry Duffy: a colourful and talented Leinster all-rounder.

Below right: Tour programme for the US and Canada adventure, 1973.

a partnership of 79 for the eighth wicket. Sadly, John Elder was adjudged lbw for nought with Anderson two adrift of a double century.

The Waringstown man was a high-class batsman, and allied to his economical off-spin and lethal work in the covers, he was a fixture in every Irish side for almost 20 years until he bowed out at Lord's in 1985. He made 3,777 runs for Ireland, which included seven centuries, two of which came in the same game against Scotland in 1976, the only Ireland batsman to achieve that feat. At the Lawn he collected medals like others collect stamps: he appeared in 15 NCU cup finals and went home with 15 winners medals. Even in the twilight of his career he was lethal – in 1993, aged 49, he bowled 22 overs in the final, taking 2-30.

The ICU had been rocked by a financial crisis in 1968, and cash problems returned again in 1975. A deputation from the union visited the provinces to appeal for assistance, which came in the form of a capitation fee levied on every player and collected by the unions. It helped the ICU over the crisis, which receded further with sponsorship, successful fixtures at Rathmines against the 1976 West Indians, 1977 Australians and Surrey in 1978 (which was also the last occasion RTE covered an Irish game live), and a lucrative entry into the English one-day competition, the Gillette Cup, in 1980. The new sources of funding allowed for more trips to the UK and for an under-19 side to take part in the International Youth Tournament every two years. This event, which saw the best young cricketers from England, Holland, Bermuda, Denmark, Canada and Ireland, became very important for bringing on young talent. Ireland beat the two English sides before losing in the 1979 final with a side that included future stars such as Mark Cohen, Jim Patterson and Davy Dennison. The tournament continued until 1997, when Ireland again finished second, losing only to an England side including future test players Robert Key, Richard Dawson and Chris Schofield. Ireland's brightest star – and only centurion – in that tournament was Ed Joyce, soon to be joining the Englishmen on the county circuit.

Inter-provincial matches were put on a formal footing in 1966 with the commencement of the Guinness Cup, the brainchild of Brian Kernan of Pembroke. This was a great step forward for ambitious players and a help to selectors, who had previously just four opportunities at most in a season to assess players at a level higher than club games. There were now 15 such games due to a division of the Leinster provinces into North and South along the course of the Liffey (though Trinity were deemed northsiders) and the NCU split into Ulster Town (Belfast, with the later addition of the north Down coast) and Ulster Country (everywhere else).

The new tournament was a great boost to Munster and North-West who now had far more opportunities to impress the Ireland selectors. North-westerners in particular had good reason to complain that they never had a good crack of the whip; only Huey, McFarlane, Shearer and Finlay had ever got a good run on the Irish team. ICU secretary Derek Scott identified another advantage North-West had in the new era – 'they were already an established entity and had players good enough to win if they could harness the talent, find a good captain and not be overawed by having to travel and play against established 'name' players. They did all three.' With Scott Huey and Roy Torrens taking 15 wickets each at less than 10, Huey captaining with such skill that he was promoted to lead Ireland that summer, and a side packed with talent such as Colhoun, Finlay and Donaghey, they won the inaugural event, and again in 1969.

Between 1970 and 1983 NCU sides won all but two titles, with the great Waringstown team providing the bulk of the Ulster Country side that won six of them.

Waringstown treble-winning team, 1973. Back row: Michael Maultsaid, Billy Houston, Barry Harrison, Gordon McKenzie, Derek Healey, Clarke Cousins, Stanley Beattie, Pete Reith, Harry Gilliland, Stanley Houston; Front row: John Irwin, Ian Harrison, Roy Harrison, Herbie Orbinson, Deryck Harrison, James Harrison Snr, Ernie McKeown, Ivan Anderson, Jim Harrison.

The inter-provincials were run on a 'time' basis until 1974 when they became 120 over matches with first innings declarations if needed. In 1977 North-West regained the title, with Ivan Lapsley recording a competition record 9-30 v Ulster Country and Ian Rankin making 95 against South Leinster to top the batting averages. Rankin is regularly named among the list of the greatest players never to play for Ireland, but he wouldn't play on Sundays when most inter-provincials were played.

The Troubles arrived in 1969 and had a serious impact on the game. Clubs, especially in nationalist areas, suffered several attacks, with serious damage caused to Brigade and City of Derry in Derry and Instonians and Cliftonville in Belfast. The destruction of their clubhouse and attacks on players forced City of Derry – who had featured a slow left-armer called John Hume, later Nobel Peace Prize winner – to withdraw from the league. The attacks reduced the number of English sides willing to travel. Of the 24 home games in the 1970s, only six were played in Ulster, with Derry and Belfast virtual 'no go' areas for much of the decade. ICU delegates from the northern unions became frustrated at the lack of fixtures in their regions and were unconvinced that sufficient effort was made to encourage foreign sides to travel there. The Guinness Cup was largely unaffected, although a regional format was introduced for one season to reduce the number of cross-border fixtures. Terrorists claimed the lives of several cricketers, including Charlie McNaul (Brigade), Harry Blair (Cregagh), Billy Elliott, John Martin and Gilbert Johnston (Armagh) and former inter-provincial player Tommy Harpur jun (RUC and Sion Mills). Armagh's Herbert Anderson, father of Ivan, was shot dead by the IRA in 1977. Shots were fired across Shane Park in Belfast during a Guinness Cup match but no-one was hurt.

Ireland v Scotland, Ayr 1974: Fred Brady (selector), Jack Short, John Elder, Roy Torrens, Simon Corlett, Stan Mitchell, David Pigot; Front: Ivan Anderson, Dermott Monteith, Alfie Linehan, Ossie Colhoun, Jim Harrison.

With the success of the Gillette Cup in England, overs cricket was seen to be the future of the game, and the NCU abandoned 'time' cricket in the late '60s. Around the same time a group of men came together in Waringstown that would dominate Ulster cricket for the next two decades. Between 1965 and 1986 Waringstown won 13 leagues and 12 cups, including eight doubles in 1967, 1970, 1971, 1973 and from 1976 to 1979. The team was backboned by as many as six brothers of the remarkable Harrison family, of whom Roy, Jim, Deryck and Garfield had distinguished Ireland careers. They were backed up by a brilliant wicketkeeper in Eddie Bushe (whose marriage to the Harrisons' sister sealed his move from Lurgan) and two quality batsmen, Anderson and Michael Reith, whose total of 44 caps would have been greater had he not spent two years in Australia in the early '70s. Reith bowled little for Ireland but was more than useful at club level, taking 7-9 in a 1971 cup match before making a century in the final against Downpatrick.

Waringstown had a great rivalry with a similarly star-studded Lisburn side, for whom Dermott Monteith was a powerful presence. A slow left-armer who was a more-than-useful right-hand batsman, Monteith played for Ireland from 1965 to 1984, when a hit-and-run driver almost took his life. The injuries he suffered meant he never played competitively again, but he left behind a monumental career record and a wealth of respect for his abilities as a bowler and tactical captain. He was at his peak in the early '70s, especially 1971 when he took 47 wickets in five matches for Ireland, including 13 each in consecutive games against Holland and Combined Services. His best analysis was 8-44 v MCC at Lord's in 1973, a season he took 46 wickets in four matches. In his 76 caps he took a record 326 wickets at 17.37, also scoring 1,712 runs at 20.62. He made his highest score for Ireland, 95 against Scotland, in his final innings.

Having impressed Middlesex captain Mike Brearley when Ireland gave the county a fright in the 1980 Gillette Cup, Monteith was invited to turn out when John Emburey and Phil Edmonds were away on test duty. He played eight games in 1981 and one more the following summer when Middlesex won the championship. A larger than life character, Monteith's autobiography A Stone in the Glasshouse is a rambunctious read about his cricketing life. In it he pays tribute to another popular, long-serving all-rounder who won 55 caps from 1953 to 1974: 'Gerry Duffy winked and blinked non-stop and talked cricket in his own indecipherable language, which included such words as malira, berlzee and oomph'.

The 1970s was a most successful decade for Ireland, who played 47 games, losing only six. Ireland had several excellent pace bowlers in the early '70s notably John Elder of Bangor and Roy Torrens of Brigade, but the arrival of Nyasaland (now Malawi)-born Simon Corlett from Oxford University gave Ireland a spearhead they hadn't had since O'Riordan was in his pomp. Corlett was one of the heroes in 1977 when Ireland beat Sussex at Pagham, taking three wickets in each innings and there at the end when the target of 200 was passed. That victory, Ireland's first over a county, had many heroes, including Monteith (3-83 and 5-38) and Chris Harte (37 and 49) but the 99 by Jack Short was a high-class innings. It was a game that spawned many anecdotes, most involving Clontarf seamer Podge Hughes. Future Pakistan captains Javed Miandad and Imran Khan were in the Sussex side and became more and more agitated as the unorthodox Hughes defied their bowlers. As the No.9 kept backing toward square leg to carve the ball to the rope, Javed screamed at Imran to knock his head effin' off!

Before the 1960s umpires had been treated poorly by clubs, some of which would not invite them in to their bars after games. Umpires were often required to wait outside for the club secretary to pay them their 5 shilling fee. In 1961 the LCU set up an umpires' sub-committee, the forerunner of the umpires' association, and in 1967 the NICUA was reconstituted in the north after a period of inactivity. Years of hard work and progress followed and training programmes introduced under the indefatigable Alan Tuffery. By the end of the century the umpiring fraternity were highly-organised and several members were rewarded with competitive fixtures in England and, in the case of Paddy O'Hara, Trevor Henry and Louis Hogan, at ICC tournaments.

The period from the late '50s up to 1970 saw the last great era of university cricket. The switch from September to June exams, and the increasing opportunities to travel and work abroad ensured that student sides could no longer challenge for the top prizes. Queen's won the league for the only time in 1959, having finished 2nd, 3rd and 4th in the preceding seasons. Their rivals in Dublin won the cup three years in a row from 1961 and the league in 1966 and 1970. The latter team, led from the front by Ireland off-spinner Michael Halliday, were unbeaten through the season, the first to do so since the 1948 side from the same club. The decisive factor was the bowling of Halliday (23 wickets), John Frankland (39) and Ronnie McCarey (30), all of whom averaged under ten.

The decade opened with the emergence of Railway Union, captained by Derek Scott, and due reward for two remarkably durable cricketers. Brendan O'Brien – 'Ginger' to all – made his senior debut in 1959 and saw service in six decades when he retired in 2001. Along the way he played 705 matches, accumulating 21,765 runs – 7,000 more than the next man – and winning 52 caps. His team-mate Niall McConnell was the second man to reach 1,000 senior wickets, his total of 1,033 later equalled by Gerry Kirwan of Clontarf.

Phoenix, the leading Leinster side in the 1970s and early 1980s, pictured in 1976. Back row: J.J. Carroll, Gordon Black, David Ensor, Brian Freer, Rod Young, Hart Cox, Ian Mullen (scorer); Middle: Gerry Murphy, Mike Halliday, Stan Mitchell, Eric Mullan, Stan Oakes. Front row: David Pigot, Rod Tilson.

Pembroke, under the captaincy of Ken Hope, won the Leinster Senior League from 1967 to 1969 with a talented team that also included Harry Hill, Alan Parker and Sandy Smith. But the Leinster scene in the '70s was dominated by a magnificent Phoenix side who won five cups in a row from 1975 to 1979, picking up three leagues and two overs leagues in the same period. The second summer that there were three trophies on offer, the scorcher that was 1975, Phoenix swept the board under the captaincy of Stan Mitchell. Their powerful batting line up was led by David Pigot, Gerry Murphy and David Ensor, while the slow bowling of Halliday (64 wickets at 9.34) and Stan Oakes (55 at 8.38) meant they bowled teams out in 20 out of 23 games. In the cup final against Leinster, Rod Young took three wickets in his 12 overs without conceding a run. Their most memorable cup win was an epic at Castle Avenue in 1976, when Leinster made 227-7, with Jack Short making 142. With one ball to go Phoenix were 226-8; Halliday hit it for four!

Michael Halliday was first capped as a student off-spinner in 1970 but went on to win a then record 93 caps before he retired in 1989. He ended with 192 wickets, and his Leinster senior record was similarly close to a milestone, ending with 983 for Phoenix and Trinity, with whom he ended his career as player/coach. Although he snapped up several five wicket hauls, his most memorable spell for Ireland was one of 4-22. It was the big talking point of the day that saw a new era for Irish cricket, with the start of competition against the counties.

ten

Limited
Progress

The invitation to play in the 1980 Gillette Cup was a godsend to the game in Ireland. The opportunity arose, after years of lobbying, because a sponsorship deal with Aer Lingus allowed the ICU to fly not just Irish players to England for games but English teams to Dublin. A regular chance to pit their skills against professionals was attractive to players, while a guaranteed slice of the competition's income ensured the financial crises of the '70s would not return.

That said, there was little optimism about our baptism in the cup – against Middlesex, the leading county at the time, and on their own ground of Lord's. Ireland had little experience of limited overs cricket – until 1980 caps were not awarded for such games. With typical élan – and contrary to all conventional thinking – Dermott Monteith decided to bat first. South African Vintcent Van der Bijl was unplayable, returning 10.5-5-12-5, but Jack Short (33) and Ivan Anderson (37) ensured Ireland passed three figures. Ireland's spinners were on top form however, and the county were reduced to 67-5 with Halliday enjoying a spell of 3-4 in 12 balls. Graham Barlow (39*) and Van der Bijl (25*) saw them home, but Halliday's 12-3-22-4 and Monteith's 11.3-4-32-0 drew lavish praise from man of the match adjudicator Jim Laker.

Middlesex came to Rathmines in 1982 with England captain and tactical guru Mike Brearley at the helm. Having made 50, he lapped the boundary where he met two of the great characters of Fingal cricket, John 'The Ranger' Mooney and his brother Tommy 'The Chink'. Brearley sat down and the trio chatted for 40 minutes. After the Middlesex man left, the Ranger was asked whether he had learned anything from the discussion. 'No', he replied, 'but he did'.

The Lord's match was a spirited and determined display, and given that it was Ireland's first appearance in the competition, gave much encouragement to dreams of giant-killing in the following years. Unfortunately that was not to be and Ireland suffered 24 consecutive defeats to the counties before beating Surrey in 2004. In 1985 Ireland were dismissed by Sussex for 39, the competition's record low score. There were several encouraging displays, however, and man of the match awards for Alf Masood (69 v Sussex 1983), Stephen Warke (77 v Surrey 1984) and Alan Lewis (4-47 and 25 v Middlesex 1991).

Lewis, the son of former international Ian, was to be a leading light in Dublin cricket for the next quarter century. A batting all-rounder, he won his first cap in 1984 at the age of 20 against West Indies. He failed to score on that occasion, but made more than 1,000 runs in Leinster cricket that summer, when his YMCA club won their first senior cup. By 2002 Lewis had eight more cup winners' medals, plus three leagues (including doubles in 1986 and 1990). He revelled in the atmosphere of the big game, and won man-of-the-match awards in six finals, where he scored three of his 15 senior centuries.

For Ireland he won a then record 121 caps, captaining on 37 occasions, but finished his career on a sour note. On the 1997 tour to England, Lewis told coach Mike Hendrick that he would be retiring after the tour. On the morning of the last game, against MCC at Lord's, Hendrick told Lewis he was dropping him to blood new players. Lewis scored 3,579 runs for Ireland, including four centuries, and also took 51 wickets. All that time he was working on his rugby refereeing, at which he is now an established international. The YMCA side of which he was part also included several others who played for Ireland, most notably the 114-times capped Angus Dunlop, plus Mark Nulty, Keith Bailey, Stewart Taylor and Jonathan Garth.

Lewis's Ireland career ran almost parallel to that of Garfield Harrison, who retired after the 1997 ICC Trophy with 118 caps, a total Lewis passed later that summer. With three

Above left: Rahul Mankad of Lurgan plays a shot in the 1984 Irish Senior Cup final.

Above right: Dermott Monteith bowls against Australia in 1977, as umpire Brian Carpenter looks on.

Right: Deryck Vincent and Enda McDermott, part of a strong Clontarf side of the 1980s and 1990s.

elder brothers already internationals, it seemed inevitable that 'Gub' would be capped. He turned into a valuable left-handed bat and off-break bowler, and was innovatively used to open the bowling at the 1994 ICC Trophy. He is one of only three men to score 2,000 runs and take 100 wickets (Alec O'Riordan and Kyle McCallan are the others) and he includes in that record a first-class century against Scotland in 1994 and the best first-class bowling of 1990 with 9-113.

The biggest development ever to hit club cricket was the inception of the Irish Senior Cup in 1982. The brainchild of Leinster CC member Murrough McDevitt, the competition brought the best 32 clubs in the country into a knockout competition, sponsored initially by Schweppes and later by Royal Liver. It was a popular and hard fought event, and led to many inter-union friendships being developed as seeding ensured that every club met someone from outside its area in the first round. The first running suffered from the reluctance to enter of the best side in Ireland at the time, Waringstown. NICC won the first final at Rathmines, beating Leinster by 91-4 to 77-9 in a 20-over game truncated by rain, with Simon Corlett winning the match award with 4-26 off 10 overs. The competition went from strength to strength, with Waringstown quickly overcoming their sniffyness and beating North in the 1983 final.

The newly-arrived professionals enjoyed the competition too, with some huge scores recorded including 169 by Chris Kuggeleijn of Pembroke, 194 by Mark Harper (Sion Mills) and 166★ by Raman Lamba (North Down). Lurgan pro Rahul Mankad (son of Indian test legend Vinoo) scored 96, 64 and 114 to help his club into the 1984 final, which they won thanks to another 130 from him. It was all too much for some in the ICU and professionals were banished from the competition in 1986. The strongest union of the era was undoubtedly the Northern, with clubs from the NCU winning 10 of the first 12 Schweppes Cups (North Down, Waringstown, Lurgan and Downpatrick winning two each), the exceptions being Phoenix (LCU) in 1986 and Donegal club St Johnston (NWCU) in 1987.

After many years without professionals, Glamorgan's John Solanky was the first of a new era in the NCU, arriving at Lisburn in 1978. In Dublin, recruitment was a hit-and-miss affair, but several top class players were to be seen in the early years, two of whom later played test cricket, Julian Weiner (Australia and Carlisle) and Chris Kuggeleijn (New Zealand and Pembroke). The first-class players began rewriting the provincial records – in 1981 South African Neville Daniels scored four centuries for Carlisle and Alan Stimpson took 91 wickets for Pembroke – but the most useful foreign recruit by a Dublin club didn't cost them a penny – at least initially.

Mohammed Afzal ('Alf') Masood was born in Lahore in 1952, and had a successful career in Pakistan (he scored three consecutive centuries against the England U19s) before emigrating to England in the mid-1970s. He came to Ireland in 1980 and found his way up to the Phoenix Park and quickly started scoring runs again. In 1982, when he made a record 1,010 senior runs, he was picked for North Leinster and broke the Guinness Cup record for runs in a season with 281, most of which came in one innings against South Leinster. Masood was on 196 not out with a run or two left to win when SL bowler Jonathan Garth – under instruction from his captain – bowled a wide which went for four. The Pakistani didn't lose much sleep over it and was soon in the Ireland team, where he remained for the next six years. When Ireland played Sussex in 1983, the opposing captain was Imran Khan, a former team-mate back home. Masood cracked 69 and Imran came up to him after he reached fifty: 'You haven't lost it at all. If you come back now you will play for us.' He hit 204★ for Phoenix against The Hills and scored a

Donemana's glittering prizes, 1988. Back row: Joe Gallagher (umpire), Lexie Kerrigan (scorer), Tom McClintock, Roger Kerr, Ian Dougherty, Desmond Curry, Barton Curry, John Devine (umpire); Front row: Robert Huey, Junior McBrine, Raymond Mitchell, James McBrine, Alan Dunn, Roy McBrine.

memorable 138 before lunch against MCC at Lord's in 1985.

A controversial figure at times, Masood was involved in some ill-fated business ventures and was forced to turn professional in the late 1980s, hiring himself out to Coleraine, Malahide and Rush, then a junior side. He finished with 40 Irish caps, scoring four centuries in 1,940 runs at 38.80, still the best average of all time. He helped an already powerful Phoenix side to three more leagues in the '80s and was man of the match when they became the first LCU side to win the Irish Senior Cup in 1986. Phoenix's rivals in the early '80s were Leinster, for whom Jack Short was a powerful batsman. The Corkman scored 6,000 runs in the ten seasons he played before emigrating to France, where he became captain of the national side. Leinster won three leagues in four seasons, with runs from Short, Brian Buttimer, David Kent, Stan Parkinson and Gerry Delany and wickets from Delany, Tom McDonnell, and Englishmen John Wills and Ernie Jones. A powerful batting line-up was the rock upon which Clontarf's six leagues in the ten years from 1991 was built. Ireland batsmen Michael Rea and Deryck Vincent recorded many century opening stands, backed up by Peter Prendergast, Ronan O'Reilly, Enda McDermott and South African pro Andre Botha, who later joined North County. McDermott, a superb tactician, was unlucky to win as few as nine caps and might have made an excellent captain of Ireland.

In the North-West, the '80s began with a controversial cup final. A few days before the game, Limavady spotted a gap in the rules and signed up Indian test star Kapil Dev for the big game. Sion Mills were incensed, even more so when he bowled throughout the first innings at one end and scored 85. When play was ended for bad light the captains and umpires were expected to come up with a time and date for continuation but the ill-feeling was such that the union had to step in and set a 4.30p.m. start.

Above: Jonathan Garth, spearhead of the talented YMCA side of the 1980s, bowls in the 1986 Leinster Senior Cup final against Malahide as umpire Stuart Daultrey casts a cold eye.

Left: John Prior receives his man of the match award from Peter Webb of sponsors Rothmans, himself a former Irish international.

Sion refused to accept their direction and when they turned up at 6.30p.m. the cup was already being supped from in Limavady. Sion were banned from the cup for the following season.

The decade belonged to just one club in the North-West, Donemana. A four-in-a-row of leagues from 1979-83 was followed by a magnificent nine-in-a-row from 1985-93. The side, who won five cups in that period, also reached two Irish Senior Cup finals but lost out to Phoenix and North Down. The village club were one of the few to shun hiring professionals, relying on a crop of excellent local talent and were almost invincible on the extraordinary sloping ground at The Holm. Their stars were all-rounders Alex 'Junior' McBrine and Desmond 'Decker' Curry. Junior won 35 caps (and twin James, incredibly, just the one), but wasn't always available for international duty. Curry had problems with the Irish selectors, too, but on his day he was the most damaging batsman in the country. His records in the north-west are phenomenal, while he also set an Irish Senior Cup record 260★ against CYM in 1998, also the highest ever made in Ireland in a limited overs game. It might have been higher had Limavady not been forced to declare after 48 overs on 373-5, as the home club had run out of balls!

Donemana apart, the North-West embraced overseas professionals with gusto. On the small grounds of the region, many batsmen created mayhem, notably West Indians Mark Harper (Sion Mills, for whom he made six centuries in 1983, and Donacloney), Everton Mattis (North Fermanagh) and Hendy Wallace (Eglinton) and Indians Kiran More (Coleraine) and Narasimha Rao (Strabane and Sion Mills). 'Bobby' Rao became naturalised and won six Irish caps in the mid-'90s.

Professionals were a contentious issue in the NCU too, with none more divisive than Delhi opener Raman Lamba. A test player who also played 32 one-day internationals for India, Lamba joined North Down in 1984. He married a local woman and returned almost every summer until his tragic death in 1998, killed while fielding in a match in Bangladesh. Lamba was an incredible batsman – he scored 1,400 in his debut season, and topped the NCU averages in 1985, 1987, 1988 and 1989, missing out on 1986 because he was touring England with India. But this skill was only eclipsed by his ability to attract the wrong sort of headlines. He was banned in India for hitting an opponent with a stump, and caused ructions when Woodvale signed him for five weeks at the end of 1986 to ensure they won promotion from Section II. He was picked for four Ireland games in 1990, with little success and less welcome from many of his team-mates and ICU officials. Lamba was not impressed that players were expected to pay for their Ireland sweater, blazer and tie, pointing out that while this might be acceptable to amateurs it was not to a professional like him. He wore an India sweater on his Irish debut and when he was given the kit in the end – with a match fee of £150 – his team-mates were furious.

While North Down didn't win any NCU trophies in his time there – Waringstown and NICC maintained their dominance with occasional interjections by Downpatrick – Lamba was not to blame for that. He was man of the match in the 1989 Irish Senior Cup final win over Donemana, but at the end of that season North Down decided to do without him and he joined Section II club Cliftonville. After a run orgy in 1990 the NCU debated banning overseas players outside Section I. Lamba and Cliftonville went to court to have the NCU declare him a local player on the grounds of marriage and residence. They lost the case and the subsequent ban saw Lamba play in the North West for Ardmore in 1991, scoring four centuries. He later joined Woodvale but returned to North Down for a couple of seasons before his death. North Down had also courted controversy when recruiting Waringstown's Michael Reith as a professional in 1980.

One of the most incredible innings ever seen in Ireland was that by Ian Botham in the Lisburn club's sesquicentenary match in 1986. With 27 to win, Botham was on 69, which meant that to score a century that he would need to score all of the next 26 runs and then hit a six with the scores level. With Ireland opening bowler John Elder to face, no-one expected even Botham to achieve it, but he hit 6, 6, 4, 4, 6 before the last ball sailed over the pavilion.

Arguably a rival to Botham's hundred was scored by Trinity student John Prior for Ireland against Warwickshire at Rathmines in 1982. In a display of power and aggression, Prior took on an attack that included England bowler Gladstone Small and despatched the ball to all corners. His 50 came up in 26 balls, his hundred in 51 balls and 51 minutes. When he was finally out for 119 he had batted just over an hour and faced 66 balls. On the strength of the innings he won a – unsuccessful – trial at Edgbaston. That was his only hundred in 37 caps from 1981-86, when he emigrated to Australia. Prior's Old Belvedere clubmate Peter O'Reilly, then just turned 18, also impressed the county, his 4-50 winning him a two-year contract. He took 30 wickets for Warwickshire's 2nd XI but never got a chance on the firsts and returned to Dublin with his action remodelled and once-blistering pace diminished.

Prior was less popular with his fellow tourists when Ireland played a Zimbabwe XI on the Irish tour there in January 1986. It was the last match of a reasonably successful programme but they had come up against a classy young bat called Graeme Hick in the previous match when he scored a rapid 155★. But he had only made 17 in the second game when he flicked the ball to Prior at square leg. Sadly the chance was spilled and Hick went on to make 309, a record innings against Ireland. Mortified by the dropped catch, Prior made 1 and 0 and the visitors lost by an innings and 67 runs.

Captaining was Michael Halliday, perhaps the most unlucky man to captain Ireland in one regard – in all 17 games he was in charge he lost 17 tosses. Ireland lost by just nine runs to India in 1986 when debutant Garth took 2-35 and scored 41, and there were other encouraging feats such as Mark Cohen's centuries against Sussex and Gloucestershire and Junior McBrine's 102 batting No.9 against Scotland. Jackson, a classy wicketkeeper who equalled Ossie Colhoun's caps total of 87, took over in due course but was replaced by Stephen Warke who captained the second tour to Zimbabwe in March 1991. Ireland won one of the two one-day games there, with all four of the longer matches drawn.

The West Indies returned in 1991, rattling up 321-4 in 60 overs, with Brian Lara falling for 4 to rookie CYM leg-spinner Conor Hoey, who took 33 wickets in his debut season. Hoey was a key member – along with Michael Rea, David O'Neill and Johnny McGrath (Trinity), Paul Stafford (Queen's) and Jimmy Ireland (UU), of the first Irish side to win an international tournament, beating Scottish and Welsh Universities and three English regional sides to win the British Universities tournament in 1986 and 1988. Ireland won the event again in 2000 thanks to innings of 114, 51★ and 81 by Trinity's Dom Joyce. University cricket has been organised since 1974, with an annual championship of up to eight teams usually won by Queen's or Trinity, although UU have won four titles and UCD one. A major blow to university cricket came in 2001 when Queen's pulled out of the NCU league, chiefly because student cricketers preferred to remain with their club rather than play for the college.

Ulster Town won the first four Guinness Cups of the 1980s, but some dismally negative cricket forced the ICU to abandon the format of one-day 'time' matches

Raman Lamba (second from right) celebrates with his North Down team-mates on winning the Irish Senior Cup final against Donemana, 1989.

and opt for 60-overs matches. With the enormous increase in international fixtures it became harder for the interpros to gain attention and the event lost credibility. There was an attempt to revitalise it by introducing a festival weekend in one union where nine of the 15 matches would be played, but the event was damaged by a foul weekend in May 1993 when all nine matches were abandoned, most without a ball bowled. Four sides ended up with one win out of five and North West won the title on bonus points.

In Leinster the senior league structure did not include automatic promotion and relegation, as in the northern unions, but there were several changes in the '80s and '90s, with the promotion of CYM in 1981 followed by three clubs from a small area of north county Dublin: The Hills (1983), North County (1990), and Rush (1995). Cork County were accepted into the league from 1996-99, their place being taken by the Munster Reds, while Laois played on a trial basis in 2005. Carlisle, a club almost entirely made up of members of the Jewish community, went out of existence after finishing league runners-up at the end of the 1998 season when their ground at Kimmage was sold. The club, who won the senior league in 1988 and 1997, made a major contribution to Irish cricket and provided the national team with Mark Cohen and the Molins brothers Jason and Greg, but the dwindling size of their community meant the disbandment of the historic club.

Cohen was one of several fine opening batsmen that Ireland had in this period, two of whom, Stephen Warke and Michael Rea, set a record partnership for any wicket of 224 against Wales in 1992 when Ireland made a brief return to College Park after 27 years. (Lewis and Harrison equalled it against Scotland two years later.) Warke, son of former international Larry, won 114 caps from 1981-96 and scored a record 4,275 runs but Rea was cut off in his prime after 52 appearances when he moved to London. Their partnership was broken in July 1993 to accommodate Justin Benson, a professional with Leicestershire who happened to be born in Dublin. While Benson had no roots in

Ireland, he moved over when released by his county and played a couple of seasons with Malahide and won 59 caps.

Benson's debut was at Clontarf against Australia, a hopelessly one-sided affair (361–3 declared played 89 all out) enlivened by blistering centuries by Matthew Hayden and Allan Border. The tourists' captain made a century in 46 balls, his second 50 coming in just 12 balls as Angus Dunlop received a savaging. Border hit five sixes off the first five balls of an over by Dunlop before miscuing the sixth for a two. These friendlies against touring sides and counties, while lucrative for the ICU, were unpopular with some players who saw themselves as bit-players in a gladiatorial slaughter. Their grievances began to be addressed by the Triple Crown tournament, which ran annually from 1993 to 2001, and the European Championship, held every two years since 1996. These events had a competitive element missing from the tourist matches and NatWest forays, playing against countries of similar standard. But an even better competitive opportunity arrived in 1994, with Ireland's acceptance into the ICC Trophy, which held out the prospect of qualification for the World Cup. It was a glittering target that was to tantalise several generations of cricketers and coaches before it would be attained.

eleven

Among the Nations of the Earth

6 July 1993 was probably the most important day in the 200-year history of Irish cricket. What happened led inexorably to a place in the 2007 World Cup finals, being the day that the International Cricket Council met at Lord's and decided to accept Ireland as an associate member of the ICC, having been proposed by England and seconded by West Indies. The decision opened the door to the ICC Trophy, the tournament that provides entry to the World Cup for the top-ranked associate members. Ireland had previously been under the aegis of the Test and County Cricket Board, having a status akin to a minor English county which allowed us to play in the English one-day competitions and receive visits from touring sides. It took some skill from ICU secretary Derek Scott to convince the authorities at Lord's that Ireland should be allowed to take its place among the nations of the earth, while still being eligible to play in English domestic competitions. The former Railway Union captain, who ran the ICU from 1974 to 1998 (having been assistant for the previous 21 years), performed his task brilliantly and Ireland were permitted to enjoy the best of both worlds.

The first benefit of the new status was an invitation to play in the 1994 ICC Trophy, held in the Kenyan capital of Nairobi, against the other associate members such as Denmark, Holland and Malaysia. Irish sides had never employed a professional coach but the Zimbabwean test player David Houghton was hired to advise on tactics for the tournament, which meant a dilution in the role for nominal coach John Wills. The fates conspired against Ireland, however, and with only three World Cup spots available, a seventh place finish was disappointing, even for a weak Irish squad. Captain Stephen Warke broke his elbow shortly before the tournament started and Decker Curry also had to return home after two games when his father died suddenly.

It was a squad already denuded of the talents of Stephen Smyth, a talented left-hand batsman from Brigade. The ICU had stipulated that players avoid contact sports such as rugby, hockey and football in the run-up to the tournament, but Smyth turned out as scrum-half in an All Ireland League match for City of Derry a week before departure and was withdrawn from the squad. It was just one episode in a controversial career that spanned the 1990s and saw him win 64 caps, including one as captain. His career ended in ignominy in September 1999 when he was banned by the ICU for five years, following an incident in a Belfast hotel during the South African Cricket Academy tour the previous month.

With the ICC Trophy held seven months after the end of the Irish season, a rusty start was expected, but victory over Papua New Guinea was achieved thanks to 50 by the new captain, Alan Lewis, and 5-29 by Conor Hoey on a drying wicket. Gibraltar were also beaten but the seeded Holland side were too strong, which meant Ireland had to beat Malaysia to progress. This was achieved thanks to 74★ by Benson and 4-18 by Hoey. The second phase taught the Irish several lessons. The United Arab Emirates side, which consisted of one local worthy and 10 Pakistanis, steamrollered Ireland as they did every other side in the tournament. The heat, humidity and altitude took its toll as a squad lacking fitness lost their last two games to Bermuda and Canada. There was one Irishman involved in the latter stages as Paddy O'Hara from the NIACUS was selected to umpire the final, which was won easily by UAE.

Ireland was invited to play in a second English one-day knockout tournament, the Benson and Hedges Cup in 1994, losing to Leicestershire. The new era of competitive cricket revitalised the national side. From the first internationals in 1855 up to 1980, every game played by the Irish side was a friendly, at least in the sporting sense. By 1996, and the commencement of the European Championship, Ireland had no less than five

The first Ireland squad to compete in the ICC Trophy, Nairobi 1994. Back row: John Wills (manager), Eddie Moore, Alan Nelson, Michael Rea, Paul McCrum, Charlie McCrum, Derek Scott (secretary); Middle row: Paddy O'Hara (umpire), Craig Mahney (psychologist), Justin Benson, Angus Dunlop, Conor Hoey, Uel Graham; Front row: Brian Millar, Paul Jackson, Garfield Harrison, Alan Lewis, Evans Dexter (president), Mark Cohen, Murray Power (scorer).

regular competitions on their agenda. The new era required far greater professionalism and the ICU took a decision they had been long-fingering for some years with the appointment of a full-time professional coach.

Mike Hendrick, a former England fast bowler, was appointed in 1995 on an initial six-month contract. A no-nonsense coach with established ideas, he discarded those unable or unwilling to make an increased commitment but is credited with bringing on some excellent young fast bowlers such as Mark Patterson, Adrian McCoubrey and Ryan Eagleson. All three also got opportunities to play in England, with Surrey, Essex and Derbyshire respectively, with limited success. Hendrick also takes credit for the stunning achievements of the summer of '96. W.G. Grace's Triple Crown notion finally came to fruition in 1993 as an annual one-day round robin (although it hasn't been staged since 2001). Ireland started magnificently, beating Scotland and England thanks to runs from Rea and Warke and wickets by Lewis and Charlie McCrum, setting up an apparent formality

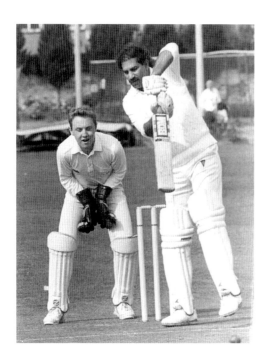

Above left: Bobby Rao plays a defensive shot for Sion Mills in the 1992 Irish Senior Cup final as Simon O'Neill (Waringstown) keeps wicket.

Above right: Programme for the 1997 ICC Trophy in Kuala Lumpur.

against the twice-beaten Welsh. But a dismal middle-order collapse saw Ireland fall 19 runs short. Ireland's only win in the tournament came in Wales in 1996, when they began with a win over England but lost the second by a similar seven-wicket margin to Scotland. Innings of 69 by Curry, 44 by captain Benson and 52* by Angus Dunlop against Wales clinched the title on run-rate, although a 'true' triple crown was never achieved.

Less than two weeks later the squad flew to Denmark for the inaugural European Championship. The trophy was achieved with three wins in the group stage against the Danes, Gibraltar and Italy, and a three-wicket win over Holland in the final. The Dutch were confined to 223-9 off their 50 overs thanks to tight bowling by Patterson, Graham, Doak and Curry. When Ireland batted Curry crashed 55 off 43 balls and man of the match Benson followed up with 79. Ireland have subsequently finished 4th, 4th, 3rd and 2nd in the Euros; the third place coming in Belfast when Ireland lost the last game to England by just one run after some dubious umpiring, while only a bowl-out defeat to the English prevented glory in 2004.

The 1996 victories were wonderful and welcome, but Hendrick knew the success of his tenure would be judged on whether World Cup qualification was secured in Malaysia the following March. The next World Cup finals were due to be held in England in 1999 and it would be a huge boost to the game in Ireland should the national side be there. It was a better prepared side than in Kenya, and there had been improvements in fitness, commitment and team spirit. Easy victories were registered against Israel and

Gibraltar and the win over the USA was described by Alan Lewis as the greatest game in Irish cricket history. Chasing 212, Ireland needed 64 off six overs when Mark Patterson walked to the wicket. The Cliftonville and Surrey paceman owed the team some runs after bowling poorly (he was a major contributor to the total of 134 wides in nine innings in the tournament) and dropping two catches, but he crashed the ball around and with the support of Garfield Harrison and Greg Molins, saw Ireland home in the final over. Defeat to Kenya put Ireland into a harder second round group, but the Dutch were beaten on run-rate and the rains saved Ireland from almost certain defeat by Bangladesh. A comfortable win over Hong Kong meant Ireland had to face the Kenyans again in the semi-final, when a win would ensure a place in the World Cup.

It was not to be. Kenya made 215-8, Paul McCrum snaffling 4-51, but Ireland's chase was not helped by a ponderous 35 off 85 balls by Benson. Wickets fell regularly and only the innings of a lifetime by Derek Heasley kept Ireland up with the rate. He fell with 38 needed in four overs and despite some hitting by Peter Gillespie, Ireland fell seven runs short. The defeat took a lot out of the team, who were now forced to play off with Scotland for third place, and the last berth in 'England 99'. It was a match too far, as Ireland's worst batting performance for years saw them dismissed for 141 after Scotland made a modest 187. Hendrick, who had lost a World Cup final with England in 1979, said Ireland's defeat was the worst feeling in his 28 years in the game.

Just 17 days later, Ireland had swapped the heat and humidity for a chilly wind blowing in off Dublin Bay. Middlesex were the first opponents in the Benson & Hedges Cup and there was a new face in the Irish line-up. The South African administrator, Ali Bacher, had earlier visited Ireland on an ICC fact-finding mission, and had prevailed upon the Springbok captain, Hansie Cronje, to come to Ireland's aid as a guest in the B&H Cup, as the rules permitted. It proved instantly successful, as Ireland recorded a first competitive win over a county. It began with pinch-hitter Decker Curry (75) smacking England bowler Angus Fraser back over his head for four in the first over, then lifting Simon Cook for a straight six into the leafy gardens of Clontarf. It ended with Cronje unbeaten on 94, and along the way McCallan (17), Lewis (34), Benson (20) and Andy Patterson (24*) chipped in to raise a formidable 281-4. Ireland bowled and fielded with passion and no Middlesex batsman made more than 34. When play ended early they still needed to make 148 off 17.4 overs with just four wickets standing, which they duly failed to achieve the following morning. The ICC Trophy had taken its toll of some players' holiday leave, however, and some key withdrawals – including man of the match Curry – meant Ireland lost the rest of the completed zonal matches.

The NCU and NWCU combined to send a Northern Ireland team to the Commonwealth Games in 1998, losing heavily to South Africa and Barbados but claiming a win when Gordon Cooke (5-35) and Ryan Eagleson (3-15) bowled out Bangladesh for 63. It was an excellent tournament featuring stars such as Tendulkar, Waugh, Ambrose, Fleming, Shoaib and Pollock but cricket was dropped from the Games in 2002.

While Ireland failed to reach the 1999 World Cup, the World Cup had no problem reaching Ireland. Hosted by England, the organisers granted fixtures to Scotland, Holland and Ireland, which meant West Indies got to play Bangladesh at Clontarf on a miserable day in May. The club ground was turned into a stadium for the day, in a remarkable feat of organisation. A crowd in excess of 2,000 turned up to spite the weather and saw Bangladesh struggle to 182 (Courtney Walsh 4-25) and the Windies pass it for three with fifties by Ridley Jacobs and Jimmy Adams.

The Ireland team celebrates the first competitive win over a county, in the 1997 Benson & Hedges Cup. Alan Lewis and Decker Curry fight over the champagne after the defeat of Middlesex.

Below left: Angus Dunlop (left) celebrates catching a Middlesex batsman as Kyle McCallan joins in.

Below right: Although Mark and Steve Waugh were members of the 2001 Australian tour party, they wore Ireland sweaters – as was their right as former internationals – on the front of the programme.

Hendrick and the ICU parted company by mutual agreement at the end of 1999, the Englishman moving to a similar role with Scotland. He was replaced by former New Zealand opening batsman Ken Rutherford, who stayed for two seasons. His baptism came in Harare, where Ireland took part in a five-team ICC Emerging Nations competition, losing to Denmark and Kenya but scoring notable wins over Scotland and Zimbabwe 'A'. The two wins were both marked by fifties by Ed Joyce, already making a career for himself with Middlesex, and tight bowling by Matt Dwyer, a veteran left-arm spinner first capped two years earlier at the age of 39. Dwyer, like the similarly overlooked-until-too-late Gerry Kirwan, had been reaping wickets by the cartload for The Hills since they arrived in senior cricket. While Kirwan won only two caps in 1983, Dwyer had 51 appearances before he stepped down in 2001. He was later appointed assistant to Rutherford's successor Adrian 'Adi' Birrell.

Rutherford was at the helm for the 2001 ICC Trophy in Toronto, the first such event Ireland had taken part in that took place during the season. To prepare, a short tour of South Africa was organised and five games played, mostly at test venues. Results were poor, but Dominick Joyce showed his class with 100★ against Gauteng Academy. Results were no better in the run-up to Toronto, although Decker Curry made his only Ireland hundred against the Earl of Arundel's XI. The team were sent off with a 72-run defeat to a side made of Leinster-based overseas players. Four of that side, Jeremy Bray, Andre Botha, Trent Johnston and Naseer Shaukat, would be part of the Ireland squad that finished runners-up in the ICC Trophy four years later.

Toronto was dismal, with Ireland's ranking and reputation slipping down the charts. The selectors took a chance with Mark Patterson (Surrey) and Ryan Eagleson (Derbyshire), two fast bowlers who had a history of problems with injury. Disastrously, both were unfit and out of form and had poor tournaments. Patterson's radar was again askew and he bowled 36 wides in 29 overs. Ed Joyce's batting blossomed and he scored four fifties in eight innings, while Dom Joyce and Jason Molins also scored heavily. The most-talked about individual performance, however, was not one recorded in a scorebook. Decker Curry was happier when opening the innings, and when he got a chance to do so against Papua New Guinea, made 95★. It was a scratchy innings however, and when Rutherford told him he was dropping him down the order for the next game, Curry exploded and pushed the New Zealander. He later apologised but left the squad and returned home. He received a short suspension but never added to his 50 caps.

Defeats to the US and Denmark were 'carried' into the second phase, where Ireland lost their first three games. Strangely, had Ireland not lost to Holland – by two runs – they might still have qualified for the semi-finals. The spate of injuries didn't help, with journalist James Fitzgerald being twice pressed into service as a substitute fielder. The last game was won, against the hosts, thanks to a century by Pembroke's Peter Davy, but it was hard to argue that Ireland deserved better than eighth place. The Triple Crown whitewash that followed saw the hapless Rutherford quit with a bitter parting shot, describing the Irish club game as 'recreational' and calling ambitions of World Cup qualification 'pie in the sky'.

In the Irish Senior Cup, the '90s saw a swing in the balance of power from North to North-West before the Dublin clubs finally got the hang of the tournament. North-West sides won six of the seven cups from 1994, with Limavady and Brigade claiming two each. Following hard on Donemana's record of nine-leagues-in-a-row came Limavady, who acquired Decker Curry in 1993 and with him swung the balance of power in the North-West. Curry's new club won six on the trot from 1994-2000 and five cups from

1997-2003. The 1997 side won both their domestic trophies and the Irish Senior Cup, with centuries in the semi-final and final by Curry, a feat he had also recorded in 1994. Strabane must have been delighted when they got him out for 23 in the 2004 final, but Ian McGregor made 89 and Limavady claimed their third cup, a feat only achieved previously by North Down and Lurgan.

Only Waringstown in 1992 and North County in 2003 have also achieved the treble of league, cup and Irish cup, and in the case of the Dublin side it was an extraordinary change in fortunes. Less than 20 years previously the club didn't even exist, but the two neighbouring junior clubs of Balrothery and Man O'War put aside an often bitter rivalry to form North County in 1985. Based in Fingal, a rural area north of the capital, the game had a development there like no other part of the Republic. While cricket died out in other parts as a game of the common man, in Fingal it retained that profile right through the late nineteenth and twentieth century, often compared to Limerick's rugby scene. Some senior clubs resisted promoting The Hills in the early '80s, but once the gates were opened a small flood ensued and virtually all expansion in Leinster in the last 20 years has been in Fingal. North County struggled for most of their first decade in senior cricket, only winning promotion out of Section B in 2000. Their rise can be traced to the election of Derek Plant as chairman in 1995. He revitalised the club, moved grounds, enticed pro Andre Botha away from Clontarf and invested heavily in some talented young players, four of whom – Paul and John Mooney, Eoin Morgan and Conor Armstrong – have played for Ireland, as has South African recruit Andre Botha.

In the north the Cliftonville club re-emerged from hibernation to win their first league since before the war in 1995. They shared the title the following season before winning it outright in 1997. Their star performers were long-time NCU pro Kamal Merchant and all-rounder Kyle McCallan. The Carrickfergus man, who travelled to the ICC Trophy in Malaysia as a member of the Irish squad but returned without playing a game, captained Ireland from 1998-2001 and became the fifth man to win 100 caps in 2003 and passed Alan Lewis's record of 121 caps in 2005. Despite being shuttled up and down the order, he has scored two centuries for Ireland and his tidy off-spin has become a crucial part of the strategy. The new century heralded a return to dominance of North Down, who won the league three years in a row and five cups out of six. The resurgence centred on Andrew White, a fabulously talented all-rounder who scored runs by the bucket load, including 1,020 in 2003, and was signed up by Northamptonshire. A powerful run machine also featured David Kennedy and father-and-son combination Robin and Ryan Haire. Another top-class run scorer was hired by Carrickfergus in the summer of 2004, and within three months of leaving Ireland was a test player with South Africa. AB de Villiers spent three months playing in Section One of the Ulster Bank Senior League, and racked up 894 runs in nine innings, including two double centuries within a week. 'I left Northern Ireland a different person and I'm convinced my time there helped me a great deal in making the South African Test side,' he told the Sunday Life's Robin Walsh.

The strangest affair of the decade was Jim Patterson suing Downpatrick for libel in 1998 after he and five team-mates left the club over a selection row. Patterson won undisclosed damages. An even sadder development was the end of Ormeau, when NICC amalgamated with Collegians to form Belfast Harlequins in 2002. Tensions with the new rugby section and relegation from the senior league in 2004 caused the cricket club to break away once again and team up with Civil Service to form a new club, Civil Service North, at Stormont. Ireland said farewell to Ormeau with a fixture against the 2001 Australians, but the weather spoilt the party and just 23 overs were possible. Queen's

Above: Jim Joyce (centre) with his some of his talented offspring Gus, Dominick, Ed and Damien.

Below left: Kyle McCallan celebrates catching Mark Ramprakash (Surrey) off his own bowling in the 2004 NatWest Trophy.

Below right: Decker Curry gives the ball some air.

University, after almost 150 years of cricket, bowed out of the league in 2000, although they have kept a presence in the universities championship.

In the inter-provincial arena, the six team format was abandoned in 1996 for four teams representing the unions plus a Development XI, who had first call on the best young players. The new side, including future Irish captains Kyle McCallan and Jason Molins, beat Leinster and the NCU in farcical 10-over thrashes and beat Munster and North-West to claim the title. The tournament went into further decline as the format was changed with bewildering frequency and the international programme expanded (there were 22 Ireland games in 1998 and 140 in the whole decade, compared to 47 in the '70s and 78 in the '80s).

The ICU continued to entice touring sides over the Irish Sea, and the increased competitiveness of the side meant some giant-killing feats. In 1994 the New Zealanders got a fright at Comber when Ireland came within six runs of their total of 233, thanks mainly to 82 by Stephen Warke. In a one-day time match at Clontarf in 1995, the West Indies rattled up 306 with a century by Chanderpaul, and had Ireland on the rack at 26-3. A rain break reduced the home side's fears of defeat but the last 22 overs were all Ireland as Smyth (95★) and Benson (74★) put together an unbroken 4th wicket stand of 161, a record for any wicket against a test touring side. The 1997 Australians won easily at Eglinton, despite 64★ by McCallan, but the following season Ireland gave a good account against South Africa at Clontarf. Chasing 289 on a cold and windy 12 July, Ireland captain Dunlop played the innings of his career to score an unbeaten century in 102 balls. The YMCA man, who captained Ireland 33 times, had set a record season aggregate for Ireland of 672 runs in 1996. That record was bettered by Smyth two years later with 703 runs – 20 of them from successive fours off Andy Bichel of Australia 'A'.

Zimbabwe won twice in 2000, despite excellent figures of 10-1-24-4 by Paul Mooney, but were annihilated by Ireland at Stormont in 2003. Mooney again bowled well, taking 2-19 off 8 overs, with his opening partner Gary Neely taking 3-30. Chasing 183 to win, Jason Molins (107★) and Jeremy Bray (67★) cruised past it in the 34th over, giving Ireland a 10-wicket win. As part of the ICC's commitment to improve the Irish game, Australia (in 1998) and South Africa (in 1999) sent A teams for ten-day tours. The Australians, who included such future superstars as Matt Hayden, Damien Martyn and Jason Gillespie, were never stretched on the tour, but a less-exalted South African side was held 2-2 in the one-day series and both three-day games were drawn. Ireland benefited from having South African star Jonty Rhodes on their side for that series, as part of a sponsorship deal with Independent News and Media that also saw Steve (1998) and Mark Waugh (2000) turn out for Ireland in competitive matches.

There was professional help for the 2004 C&G Trophy, with South African state player Gerald Dros hired for the first round game against Hertfordshire (played in August 2003) which saw an Irish record total of 387-4, the tenth highest in the history of the competition. Molins made 84, Dros 124 and man of the match Botha 139 and 4-37. Ireland had won nine matches on the trot when Surrey turned up at Clontarf for the next round in May 2004. With Andre Botha and Andrew White taking three wickets each, the reigning English one-day league champions were bowled out for 261. It wasn't an out-of-sight score, but to beat it Ireland would have to score more than they ever had against a professional side in the competition. As against Zimbabwe, the Phoenix clubmates of Bray and Molins were positive and stayed together until the hundred was raised, both making fifties. Dros added 45 but it was Gillespie (28), White (20★) and McCallan (17★) who saw Ireland home, with White winning the man of the match

Niall O'Brien and Andrew White celebrate the six-wicket defeat of West Indies in 2004.

award. It had been a long 25 years since Ireland had first entered the event and the first win over a first-class county was sweet – and showed how much progress had been made. Bray (76), Gillespie (56) and White (44) set a new record of 263-8 in the next round against Northamptonshire, but the county won with eight overs to spare.

Further notice was served of the new-found power and confidence of the Irish team when a third historic victory over the West Indies was recorded two weeks later. This time the tourists set a target of 293, but positive batting all the way down the order saw victory clinched with more than three overs left. Molins, Bray and Niall O'Brien all made 50s and the middle order of Gillespie and White acted as 'finishers'. A measure of Ireland's increased stature was the less-patronising approach taken by the foreign media who had piled on the Guinness and Leprechauns analogies in 1969.

Irish cricket's investment in underage coaching and competition paid off in style with a heartening series of successes by underage sides in the new century. The European Cricket Council organise a series of European Championships, which Ireland's Under-19s won in 2000, 2003 and 2004, and Under-17s in 2001, 2002 and 2005. In the younger categories Ireland were unbeatable, winning the Under-15 title every year since 2000 and the Under-13 each year since it began in 2001. While he never reached these

West Indian great Clive Lloyd protects himself from the elements at Clontarf during the 1999 World Cup.

heights, the best known Irish schoolboy cricketer of the twenty-first century was Phoenix under 13s and Hollywood actor Colin Farrell.

The Under-19s qualified for three biennial World Cups, which were formidable events, including all the test countries and some players who had played at full international level. Ireland finished 13th in South Africa in 1998 and 12th in India in 2000, but the performance in Bangladesh in 2004 showed progress. Chasing 266 to win against eventual finalists West Indies, Ireland went down by just six runs thanks to 95 by Kevin O'Brien, whose father Brendan and brother Niall have played for Ireland. In the plate semi-final Ireland were unlucky to have to face Australia who racked up 340-5, but again a huge total held no fears. Ireland made 291-9, with 65 by Eoin Morgan who had made a century earlier in the tournament. They have also qualified for the next Youth World Cup, to be held in Sri Lanka in March 2006.

For the full Ireland team, another new annual competition began in 2004, the ICC Intercontinental Trophy, which offered three-day matches rated first-class for the associate members. After beating Holland by an innings in Deventer (with White scoring 152★ on his first-class debut) Ireland needed only to draw with Scotland to qualify for the final tournament in Sharjah. A Clontarf green-top wicket didn't help, but in truth Ireland didn't bat well enough after establishing a small lead on first innings and the Scots qualified for the finals, where they beat Kenya and Canada to win the cup. It was a disappointing end to a phenomenal season and a missed opportunity to keep the squad together over the winter before the ICC Trophy. But it reminded the Ireland players that nothing was as important as qualification for the World Cup, and they would never have a better chance to do so than on home turf in July 2005.

twelve

Five
World Cups

Women have played an important role in the development of cricket, most notably the first over arm bowler Christina Willes, who adopted the style trying to avoid her billowing skirt in the early eighteenth century. For a time it was a novelty, but in time the game developed into a hard-fought competitive international sport with a character of its own. Irish women qualified for the World Cup finals long before the men even came close to doing so – and have now played in five successive tournaments. It is remarkable progress for a sport that was almost moribund just thirty years ago.

The first evidence of women's cricket in Ireland was a report of a match played in July 1884 in the grounds of Camus Rectory, near Strabane. Eleven Ladies, led by Miss Claudine Humphrey's, beat a team of men by one wicket. Over the next decades there were several references in the press to games between schoolboys and schoolgirls, or novelty games between men and women in which the males batted with broomsticks or stumps. In July 1908 an Irish Schoolgirls v English Schoolgirls game was played at Woodbrook, but the result has not survived.

Three girls' schools – Sion Hill, Holy Faith, Glasnevin and Glengara – continued to play but the women's game only took off after a letter by George Bonass, president of the Leinster Cricket Union, was printed in The Irish Times in April 1936. Bonass wrote that he had seen some excellent cricket in England between women's sides and wondered where all the Irish women cricketers were. Such was the response that Bonass organised a charity match for the Pembroke ground at Sydney Parade in between Miss Deirdre Ennis's XI and Miss Isolda Howard's XI, at which a collection was taken for the Children's Sunshine Home.

Isolda Howard was a giant of Irish women's cricket for most of the 20th century. She was still a pupil at Muckross when Bonass prevailed on her to organise a team for the inaugural match. Two years later she founded the Leinster Women's Cricket Union and went on to sit on its committee for the next 38 years on behalf of Leinster CC. Fellow international Clarissa Pilkington described her thus: 'As a left-arm bowler she kept immaculate line and length and could get a bit of spin on the ball. She was a most determined bat, capable of making runs and well able to break the hearts of opposing bowlers if it became necessary to play out time. During her career she never missed an Inter-provincial or International match. Her grand finale should have been to captain Ireland against New Zealand in Belfast 1966, but the rain put paid to that, for not a ball was bowled. Unfortunately records were not kept in the early days so her triumphs must go unrecorded.'

The 1936 game gave an impetus to women's cricket, gathering together mostly schoolgirls from Muckross, Wesley and Alexandra Colleges. Miss Ennis's XI declared at 109-4, when her bowlers, bowling underarm, skittled their opponents for 59. Among the pioneers that day were two hockey internationals, Clare Parsons and Evie O'Kelly, and Betty Magee, daughter of a celebrated cricket and rugby family.

Leinster continued to play against women's sides got up by other clubs and in 1938 the LWCU was founded by Civil Service, Dartry, Carlisle, Bellshire, Rush and Leinster. Magee presented a trophy for a league which was won by Leinster. An inter-provincial game was organised for Cork on 10 September 1939 but the outbreak of World War II put paid to that. The war and petrol shortages caused serious damage to the nascent organisation, and half the original member clubs folded. Over the next few years Trinity, Clontarf and Railway Union joined up but Leinster and Civil Service folded.

The Trinity club was limited by the small number of women who studied there, but there was a great influx of English students after the war and the game took off.

Dublin University, 1951. Back: Stephanie de Ranzi, unknown, Barbara Robertson, Nora Henderson, Sheila Lyon, Seated: Inez Cuthbert, Jennifer Pollard, Fodhla Burnell, unknown; Front: Kitty Richardson, Clarissa Crawford.

Leinster v Ulster, 1962. Isolda Howard is in the middle of the front row.

Stella Owens: glorious career cut short by injury.

Irish squad that toured Trinidad and Tobago, 1986. Back row: Rachel Hardiman, Pam Trohear, Stella Owens, Karen Smyth, Alice Stanton, Gwynneth Smith, Miriam Grealey, Sonia Reamsbottom; Front row: Saibh Young, Ann Murray, Lily Owens, Mary Pat Moore, Donna Armstrong, Susan Bray, Grainne Clancy.

Although they were not allowed to play in College Park, guided by male international Sonny Hool they turned into a fine team with Clarissa Crawford, Gladys Ruddock and Fodhla Burnell to the fore, winning the league in 1947, 1949 and 1951.

Clarissa Crawford, later Pilkington, was born in Ulster but stayed in Dublin after graduating from Trinity. She worked for the university as warden of Trinity Hall, the residences in Dartry, which was where the women's club was based. A regular Ireland player through the 1940s and 1950s, she returned to the game in the 1970s as an administrator and a key figure in schoolgirl coaching. She also coached Trinity's women into the twenty-first century when she retired at the age of 80. Should a player fail to turn up, Pilkington would usually make up the numbers and shame those a quarter her age with her textbook technique.

Women's cricket was slower to take hold in Ulster, but did so when Paula Furniss, a leading player at Trinity, returned home full of enthusiasm. The North-West Women's Cricket Union and the Northern Women's Cricket Union of Ireland were set up shortly afterwards and sides formed at Belfast, Holywood, Lisburn, Muckamore and Newtownards. With six clubs from the North-West, an Ulster side was established and an inter-provincial series against Leinster ran from 1947 to 1967.

Although there was no national body, there was an Irish side for almost two decades who played county and representative sides from England, where both Leinster and Ulster

'Ice maidens'. This photograph of Lily Owens, Annie Murray and Rita Kenny won first prize in Sandymount Arts Week photography competition, 1985.

toured. Standards of play were improving all the time and the leading players in this era were Marie Coffey (Clontarf), Ivy Hadden (Dartry) and Clarissa Crawford (Trinity). The leading Northern woman was Cherry Britton, but she emigrated to Australia where she became a state player and just missed out on test selection.

13 August 1966 was to be a red-letter day in Irish women's cricket history, as the first international was organised against New Zealand at Belfast. Northern cricket was strong at the time, and more than half of the side came from north of the border: Rosalind Armstrong, Cherry Britton, Joyce McIlwrath, Maura Smyth, Margaret Monaghan (all Belfast CC) and Annette Patton (Sion Mills). The team was made up by five women from Dublin: Isolda Howard (Leinster, captain), Gladys Ruddock, Ivy Hadden, Heather Squire and Beryl Squire. However, torrential rain caused the match to be abandoned without a ball bowled. With only three other countries playing women's cricket at the time, the chance to play another international would not come around for another two decades.

Interest in Leinster waned towards the end of the 1960s and for a time only Clontarf and Trinity played and those clubs died out completely by 1970. The Troubles forced an end to women's cricket in the north in 1972, and although it was revived at Belfast CC in the late 1970s, there was just one women's team who played friendlies against men's sides.

The game in Dublin began anew when an American woman, Barbara Schmidt, and

Jenny Halliday, wife of Michael, organised a game for Trinity Week in 1975 between the university and a team from Phoenix. This spark, like that ignited by Bonass 40 years earlier, set off a bushfire of interest and the following season the LWCU was reactivated and a seven-team league commenced, the title shared by Clontarf and Leinster. Large numbers of girls and women began turning up at cricket clubs – one surge in interest followed a report on Gay Byrne's radio programme – and sponsors were secured by Schmidt for what became the Tyler Cup. The Clontarf club surfed this new wave better than anyone and they swept the trophy board for much of the next decade. Their success was built on some brilliant players, notably Mary and Ann Murray, Tracey Skoyles, Susan Bray, and the Owens sisters Stella and Lily.

Stella Owens was the biggest star in Irish women's cricket for a decade. Growing up next to Castle Avenue, she was a regular on the schoolboy sides in Clontarf until the branch changed the rules to exclude girls. She was player of the match in the women's senior cup final in 1977 – at the age of 11. Her pace was lethal in the women's game and her ability to cut and swing the ball was envied by many experienced male players. She played in the first women's internationals at 17 and was selected to play alongside ten men for UCD in the 1985 intervarsities tournament, holding her own with several international and interprovincial players. Injuries cut her career short – she stopped bowling at the age of 23 and retired completely at 28 – but her 35 Irish caps saw her score 697 runs at 24 and take 19 wickets at 28.4.

Moves towards an international dimension began in 1978 when the Scotland women travelled over for a short tour, but they were hammered by selections of South and North Leinster and never returned. Schoolgirls cricket got under way in 1979 thanks mainly to the efforts of Bob Whiteside and Clarissa Pilkington, eight teams played in the first cup competition, won by Whiteside's charges in King's Hospital. When the interprovincial series between Leinster and Ulster resumed in 1980 – with the addition of Munster – the recovery was almost complete.

Isolda Howard had kept the Irish flag flying in the outside world, attending cricket week at Malvern in England every year and making an annual pilgrimage to the WCA Annual General Meeting, even through the inactive years. So it was entirely natural that she be invited to become the first President of the IWCU on its foundation in 1982. Her international dream, foiled by the rains in 1966, came to fruition when Pilkington received an invitation from Holland for an Irish side to take part in a quadrangular tournament the following August. The IWCU was formed to administer the game on an all Ireland basis, and the team was selected for the Dutch tournament, to be coached by former Ireland captain Noel Mahony and managed by Mary Sharp of Pembroke. Sharp was to play an enormous role as an administrator over the next twenty years, being at the heart of the IWCU's progress before becoming the first female Secretary of the Leinster Cricket Union (her husband Michael has been Secretary of the Junior Branch for a quarter of a century) and president of Pembroke CC. This was a rare honour for a woman only preceded in Dublin by Barbara Schmidt at Phoenix in 1990, although Mrs Margaret Waring – the young widow of Holt – was President of Waringstown for many years and represented them on the NCU committee. She was elected president of the NCU for 1954-55.

The debut tournament was a spectacular success for Ireland, with two wins – over Young Holland and Denmark – and one defeat, to Holland. Stella Owens, aged 17, was named Woman of the Series after scoring 85* against the Dutch junior side and taking 3-14 against Denmark. The following season Ireland hosted the Young England side in a three-match series, and while all the games were lost, progress was obvious against a team featuring several Test players.

In 1986 the IWCU hosted a quadrangular tournament with Holland, Denmark and Young England – won by the latter – and toured Trinidad and Tobago in October 1986. Another important stage in Ireland's development was the visit of the Australians to Ormeau and Trinity in 1987. The three games resulted in heavy defeats -- by 110, 123 and 105 runs -- but the Irish learnt much from the professionalism of the visitors and the spectators had their eyes opened to the standard of women's cricket at the top level. Less than five years after the formation of the IWCU the Irish game was recognised with an invitation to the fourth Women's World Cup in Perth, Australia. A resourceful group raised funds but the players were still asked to pay a large sum to represent their country. Only five countries took part in December 1988, the three established sides of England, Australia and New Zealand, plus Holland and Ireland, and each team played the other twice. The games were of 60 overs duration, which was quite a challenge for the Irish women used to playing 20- and 40-over cricket. With former Irish national coach Noel Mahony at the helm, one of their ambitions was to bat out their overs against the stronger sides, which they did six times out of eight, and were never bowled out earlier than the 57th over. Ireland lost those games heavily – Australia twice by ten wickets – but won both against the Dutch, thanks to fine all-round play by Stella Owens (66, 2-8 off 7 overs and 3-31). Her clubmate Anne Murray made a memorable 58 against England and 44 v Holland. In the third-place playoff Ireland restricted New Zealand to 208-6 but, despite 54 by captain Mary Pat Moore and 36 by Murray, Ireland lost by 70 runs.

In 1993 the World Cup was held in England, with Brendan O'Brien taking over from Mahony. Eight sides took part and hopes were high as the event was held during the Irish season and in conditions similar to home. Ireland were able to call on a large group of supporters, most notably a group called The Six Pack who were an early example of Barmy Army-style supporting. Ireland slipped to a disappointing fifth, behind newcomers India, but ahead of West Indies and Denmark. The captaincy was returned to Moore, who was then living in England and playing for Yorkshire, and the side won two out of seven games, with excellent batting by Miriam Grealey (179 runs at 44.75), Sonia Reamsbottom (211 at 30.14) and Moore (189 at 31.50). Susan Bray had a good tournament, conceding little more than two an over in her 9-174 off 80 overs.

There were some good performances, including a record 234-6 off 60 overs against Denmark with a partnership of 96 by Grealey (63★) and Stella Owens (61), and Bray returning an analysis of 12-5-22-3. The defeat against Australia was spirited, with the world champions restricted to 194-8 and Ireland ending on 145-5 thanks to 44★ and 12-4-18-2 by New Zealand-born all-rounder Catherine O'Neill. In five meetings between the nations at World Cups it is the only one not to finish in a ten-wicket win for the Aussies.

Miriam Grealey, a Donegal native who played with the YMCA club in Dublin, was to have a long career in an Ireland sweater. First capped against Australia in 1987, she finally bowed out after the 2005 World Cup at the age of 39, appearing in four World Cups and collecting 80 caps. An off-spinner and powerful batswoman, she scored 1,412 one-day international runs including a century against Pakistan at Rush in 2000.

The biennial European Championship, which began in 1989, usually saw Ireland finish second behind England. The 1995 event was held in Dublin and despite 46 by Grealey and 37 by Lily Owens on her finale the English won by 7 wickets. Mary Pat Moore became Ireland's first centurion when she made 114★ batting for 149 balls against Denmark at the Europeans, held in Dublin in 1995. Moore batted for 149 balls against

Denmark at Park Avenue and setting a record opening stand of 181 with Anne Linehan (74) as Ireland scored 238-2. The pair added 99 in the next game, against Holland, but they were both dismissed with just four on the board in the final against England, Linehan falling to the first ball of the match. Lily Owens (37) and Grealey (46) staged a revival with 71 in 22 overs, but 150-8 was never enough against the world champions. Susan Bray was magnificent, conceding just 14 runs off her ten overs and England were rattled at 18-2 off 11 overs, but Barbara Daniels, Jane Smit and Karen Smithies saw them home.

For the 1997 World Cup, held in India, the competition expanded to 11 teams with the addition of Sri Lanka, Pakistan and South Africa. Again Ireland slipped back, ending with a ranking of seventh. Of the six games, the Australians were avoided with the help of torrential rain, and there were heavy defeats to South Africa, New Zealand and England, for whom Claire Edwards made a world record 173★. Denmark were easily overcome, while Pakistan were hammered by 182 runs thanks to a second fifty by Grealey and merciless bowling by O'Neill (10-5-10-4) and Adele Spence (5-2-4-3). Grealey described the game as 'an awesome experience' for the Irish women, unused to playing in front on 15,000 people!

A further boost was received with the IWCC decision to award test status to Ireland's first – and so far only – four-day match against Pakistan in College Park in 2000. It was a total mismatch, completed in two days, after the visitors were bowled out for 53 (Barbara McDonald 12-6-9-3, Saibh Young 10-9-1-0, Catherine O'Neill 13.4-7-15-3 and Ciara Metcalfe 12-3-26-4) and 86 (Isobel Joyce 11.1-5-21-6, O'Neill 14-7-12-3). Ireland rattled up 193-3 before declaring, with fifties for Kiwi-born Karen Young and Caitriona Beggs of Malahide. Much of the media interest surrounded the Pakistani Sajjida Shah, aged 12, who made 2 and 0. Four years later Shah made 98 in a test against West Indies.

The 2000 World Cup, held in New Zealand, was slimmed down to eight sides, being the top eight finishers from the previous tournament. The squad, who usually had to pay a chunk of their fares for World Cups, received a marvellous boost from a generous senior member of the IWCU. This lady had indicated she would bequeath £10,000 to women's cricket, but with a merger with the ICU in the wind she decided to bring forward the donation. Ireland were coached by former South Leinster bowler John Wills, but a weak bowling attack ensured only one win was recorded, against Holland, when Beggs made 66★ and Linehan 54. Most disappointing was a 10 run defeat to Sri Lanka when they had bowled them out for 129. A fine fielding performance – there were five run outs – and tight bowling by O'Neill, Grealey and Isobel Joyce was ruined by chaotic batting. Four runs outs set the tone and only Karen Young (30) and Linehan (20) showed resistance. The highlight of the tournament was the opening overs against India, when they were reduced to 4-3, only to recover to 199. Ireland chased all the way down the order but lost by 30 runs. The final placing of sixth was doubly disappointing because it meant Ireland had to pre-qualify for the next World Cup.

In February 2001 the Irish Women's Cricket Union's 20-year life span came to an end when it amalgamated with the ICU under pressure from the Sports Council in the Republic. The move, Wills said at the time, would give the women access to facilities, coaching, travel funding and ground allocation. 'It's hopeless. We have no right, no power, to go to a club and say we need a ground for internationals. It will formalise ground allocation both for internationals and junior internationals.'

After the gloom of the 2000 World Cup, the 2001 Europeans were a highpoint in the Irish women's game, with a stunning victory over England in the final at Reading. Ireland's total of 116 looked paltry, with Beggs' 35 the highest contribution as they

Above: Caitriona Beggs in action against Australia during the 2000 World Cup.

Below left: Miriam Grealey: played for Ireland at four World Cups.

Above right: Clarissa Pilkington with Ireland captain Lily Owens, 1986.

collapsed from 93-3. At 48-3 in reply the English were cruising, but veteran Saibh Young took a hat-trick in her first over and Grealey took a wicket in the next to leave the score 48-7, which quickly became 60 all out. The Irish squad were surprised to receive mementos with the word 'England' engraved upon them! It was a great performance after the disappointment of the World Cup in New Zealand, and new captain Nikki Squire and coach Richard Davies won much praise for their work with a young squad. Unfortunately much of the momentum was lost when both resigned within six months, Davies becoming frustrated when the resources to develop the squad were not forthcoming and he was soon followed by Squire.

The first IWCC Trophy took place in Holland in 2003, with two places in the World Cup up for grabs and Railway Union's Peter Johnston as coach. Ireland justified favouritism by winning all five of their games, with the bowling of O'Neill, McDonald and Isobel Joyce giving most encouragement while the evergreen Grealey and Beggs made the runs.

The 2005 World Cup in South Africa only continued the gradual downward slide in rankings and standards that had been evident since the first clutch of talented players retired in the late '80s and early '90s. While the rest of the world had improved and new nations adopted the game, the gap between the best and Ireland had widened. Off the pitch, some of the players were in open revolt with coach Johnston and he jumped before he was pushed at the end of the campaign. Captain Clare Shillington was also a casualty of a disastrous tournament which saw five defeats and two games abandoned because of rain, albeit those in which hopes of a win were entertained. Sides such as India and West Indies, who were much later taking to the game than Ireland, handed out humiliating defeats. Not one player averaged 20 and no-one made even a 40. One batswoman scored just 6 off 78 balls against England and 7 off 78 against New Zealand. The eighth-place finish provoked much debate on their return, but shedding the coach and captain would not solve the underlying problem of the lack of quality players and insufficient opportunity to play against top sides. The disappearance of the women's structure into the ICU is also blamed for reducing the status of the game. There are hopes that the ICU's new-found riches might trickle down into funding for winter tours to help keep pace with the international game, but so far few advantages seem to have accrued to women's cricket.

There is hope for the future, with a revival of activity in the North and the inauguration of a league in the North-West with Creevedonnell the leading club. In Leinster the three division league features 20 teams from 14 clubs, while the Irish women's side play in the eighth division of the men's Leinster league, which gives them an opportunity to play together regularly, albeit in 40-over games.

Ulster coach and former international Donna Armstrong sees hope for the future in the province 'It may not be at its strongest at senior level, but the encouraging thing is that it's beginning to take hold within the schools,' she says. 'Dozens of schools are now playing cricket instead of the traditional rounders – for example over 200 girls are playing cricket at Methodist College in Belfast alone.' Fifteen schools with 42 teams compete in the Leinster schools competitions and an Under-17 inter-provincial series began in 2005. Grealey has coached the Development and Under-21 sides for four years and sees progress: 'Clubs like Leinster, Merrion, Clontarf and Rush have a youth policy and they have loads of kids playing. I'll need to help two or three of them to come on to the Irish scene in the next couple of years when the likes of Annie Linehan, Caitriona Beggs and Barbara McDonald are nearing retirement. We need to have more players coming through from Ulster though.'

The 2005 Ireland side pose for photos before they leave for South Africa.

The strength in Irish women's cricket has never come from numbers, but from determined, organised people like Isolda Howard, Clarissa Pilkington, Marie Coffey, Mary Pat Moore, Miriam Grealey, Stella Owens, Mary Sharp, Noel Mahony, Ursula Lewis, Siobhan McBennett, Elaine Coburn, Donna Armstrong and Maureen Joyce. These women and men dragged women's cricket up from a fanciful notion on a newspaper letters page to a place in the top ten in the world. It has always been a struggle, and will continue to be, but their passion for the game will ensure Irish women's cricket continues to progress.

thirteen

Rejoyce!

When ICU secretary John Wright bent to pick up his post one morning in January 2002, he noticed the colourful stamps with the words 'South Africa' printed on them. He might not have remarked upon it at the time – he was getting plenty of letters from exotic places just then – but that moment put in train a change in fortunes for the Irish game that ended with qualification for the 2007 World Cup.

Forty-one year old Adrian Birrell, known as Adi, was coach of Eastern Province in South Africa, where he had played 45 first-class games as a leg-spinning all-rounder. His father Harry had also played for EP, as well as Oxford University and Rhodesia. Adi continued on the province's coaching staff and was heavily involved in the development of cricket in the townships. His impressive CV also included a spell running the South African Academy and coaching the under-19 national side. While there were 40 applications for the job, and a shortlist of five that included a couple of very prominent names, the ICU was confident that in Birrell they had the man to transform Irish cricket.

He inherited a side despondent after their performances in Toronto and bereft of its greatest player. He set about revitalising the remnants of that squad – half of that 14 played in the 2005 ICC Trophy, and all were far better players – and identifying likely talents around the clubs. He also inherited, in Ian Johnston, Brian Buttimer and Willie Wilson three selectors with a deep knowledge and passion for the game. Some of the selections made by the quartet were unpopular: the capping of wicketkeeper Niall O'Brien in 2002 was widely criticised but within a year he had scored a century and been hired by Kent.

Birrell was fortunate, too, that the Irish economy had been going through an unprecedented boom. From the mid-'90s, many young men from around the world had made their way to Dublin in search of employment and our fabled 'craic'. Some sold their skills as cricketers; four of them decided to stay on and commit to the Irish game and the women they had met. The quartet of Jeremy Bray, Trent Johnston, Andre Botha and Naseer Shaukat each provided a handful of pieces that helped Birrell complete the jigsaw.

All four had played top-class domestic cricket in their native lands: Bray and Johnston for New South Wales, Botha for Griqualand West in South Africa and Shaukat for Faisalabad in Pakistan. Bray had just broken into the NSW squad, playing against New Zealand in 1997, when his girlfriend Geraldine received news that her father was seriously ill. The pair upped and travelled to Ireland, where they have lived ever since. Based in Kilkenny, he travelled up at weekends to play for Phoenix, and soon became the most prolific player ever seen in the LCU, beating even Masood's records. He four times passed 1,000 runs in a season in senior club games, setting a new record 1,273 in 2000. In the seven seasons up to the end of 2004, he had scored 6,776 runs in 122 innings, an average of 71.32, well clear of his nearest rivals Botha (51.25) and Masood (51.22). He made a fifty or hundred every second trip to the crease and usually made his runs at a cracking pace.

Bray had been identified by the ICU early in his Irish career and encouraged to qualify. He was first capped in late 2002 against Berkshire and made his first century for Ireland against Denmark the following year. He had played from the age of 12 with Trent Johnston, who first came to Ireland in 1995, initially as a pro with Carlisle but later playing for Leinster and Clontarf. Johnston was first capped against Surrey in the epic C&G Trophy win in 2004, and makes his living as logistics manager with Edun Apparel, the clothing firm run by U2 singer Bono and his wife Ali Hewson.

Andre Botha was another well-travelled pro, playing with Clontarf from 1994 to 2000 when the lure of North County proved impossible to resist. He, too, was a prolific

Trent Johnston (right) has a word in the ear of Adi Birrell.

club player, overshadowed only by Bray. He won a lot more club honours than the Australian, however, none sweeter than the 2001, 2003 and 2005 Irish Senior Cups.

The foreign-born players were added to the squad over the three years Birrell had to prepare for the trophy, and Gordon Cooke of Brigade was recalled after a spell on the sidelines. Peter Gillespie, first picked as a fast bowler, won a recall as a batsman after Toronto and remained in the side. To the mix was added Eoin Morgan, a precocious young man from north county Dublin whose talents were spotted early on by Middlesex who contracted him as soon as he reached the age of 16. With a couple of Middlesex 2nd XI centuries under his belt, Morgan was first capped by Ireland in 2003, three weeks short of his seventeenth birthday. At the time he was the youngest-ever international, beating David Trotter's record set in 1875, but Greg Thompson was two months younger when he played against MCC in 2004.

Middlesex's interest in Irish players had been sparked by the glorious success of Ed Joyce, whose performances and progress over seven seasons had taken him to the brink of England selection. One of a Merrion family awash with cricket talent (brothers Gus and Dominick, and sisters Cecilia and Isobel played for Ireland), Joyce had been spotted as an exceptional player from an early age. Rising through the youth ranks, he recorded centuries at schools, university and under-19 level and first played for Ireland

Jeremy Bray and Jason Molins flicker to and fro.

in the 1997 Triple Crown. He made his county 1st XI debut in September 1999, but his studies at Trinity meant he could only travel to Lord's for the second half of each season. When he started playing full-time, he quickly blossomed and made 1,000 runs in each of his first four full seasons, in 2005 doing so faster than anyone else. His batting drew comparisons with fellow left-handers Graeme Pollock, David Gower and Graham Thorpe, his easy style suited to rapid accumulation of runs allied to a developing ability to dominate attacks. Australian legend Shane Warne was the most notable of his admirers, commenting that he was the best batsman he had seen in England in 2005.

His availability for the ICC Trophy – four years after his last Irish appearance, in Toronto – was a huge bonus for Birrell. His county were happy to accommodate him, unlike Niall O'Brien who felt pressure from Kent and unhappily withdrew his name from consideration. 'Kent were prepared to bring in another keeper to cover for me while I was away with Ireland, but they made it clear to me that if my replacement did a good job they couldn't guarantee I would get my place back', he explained. The

Ed Joyce prepares to bat for Middlesex at Bristol in 2000. Also pictured are Mike Gatting (coach), Mark Ramprakash and Justin Langer.

tendency for the best Irish players to take up contracts in England was always likely to end in tears, although when Andrew White secured a deal with Northamptonshire he had a clause inserted that he be released for the ICC Trophy.

With Jeremy Bray pressed into service as wicketkeeper, the squad began to take shape. Early friendlies saw Morgan and Dom Joyce in the runs, while Botha scored 85 and took 4-39 against Warwickshire. Morgan (59) was man of the match in the C&G defeat to Yorkshire, when Gillespie also made a fifty. Two games against MCC produced easy wins, with Gillespie making the fastest hundred ever scored for Ireland, eclipsing John Prior's 1982 innings. Gillespie faced just 47 balls for his 102* at Bangor, raising his century with a six over deep backward square off the last ball of the innings. He hit 8 fours and 6 sixes in an innings that marked his eighty-seventh cap, equalling Colhoun's record by a north-westerner.

A couple of niggles to squad members meant Ireland fielded six players who were not in the ICC party. With immaculate timing, Conor Armstrong scored 55 and 90 to remind the selectors of his talent. Unluckiest of all was John Mooney, a regular cap over the previous two years and the best fielder in the side. The selectors nominated three players to stand by for the tournament; naturalised South African Ralph Coetzee to cover the spinners White and McCallan, Stephen Ogilby of Cheshire as reserve keeper and Mooney to cover all other eventualities.

They were the best-prepared Irish squad to enter an international tournament, and the

Above left: Jason Molins, Ireland captain.

Above right: The programme for 2005 ICC Trophy.

Left: Andre Botha of North County lifts the Irish Senior Cup in 2003.

most committed. For two years captain Jason Molins, a fund manager based in London, would hop on his Vespa every Friday and buzz out to Heathrow for a flight home to play for Phoenix. The 30-man squad practised almost every weekend over the winter, working with Birrell on improving techniques and nailing down what Molins called 'the one percenters that might make a difference'. Aware that conditions for the ICC Trophy might be inclement, a bucket of water was used at indoor nets to practise wet ball bowling. Eye specialists were called in, detailed research was undertaken into the opposition and the grounds at which they would play them.

All the planning ended on 1 July, when Molins and Bray walked out to bat at Stormont against Bermuda. The partnership they formed had been one of the key elements in Ireland's improvements: the three big wins of recent seasons – against Zimbabwe, Surrey and West Indies – had been built upon opening stands of 183★, 103 and 111 respectively. It was not to be that day, however, as Molins was run out for 3 and Ireland slipped to 62-3. The Middlesex pair of Joyce and Morgan came to the rescue with a stunning stand of 170, in which Morgan outscored his senior partner with 93. The Bermuda coach, former West Indian batsman Gus Logie said afterwards 'Joyce is a great player. I was more impressed with the fellow Eoin Morgan though.' Joyce went onto make his first international century off 89 balls as Ireland racked up 315-8, which was far too many for Bermuda.

Against Uganda at Comber the following day Ireland again got off to a poor start, losing three wickets reaching 60, before the middle order of Joyce (40), Morgan (49), White (45) and Johnston (39) stabilised the innings. A total of 231 was less than they might have hoped for, but Paul Mooney got into his rhythm immediately and soon had the Africans in disarray at 30-7. A last wicket stand almost doubled Uganda's total to 104 with Mooney man of the match with 10-4-10-3.

It was back to Stormont for the United Arab Emirates game and this time Ireland inserted the opposition. Mooney again struck early but the UAE rallied before Johnston returned to bowl them out for 230. In what was becoming a disturbing pattern, Ireland's top order went cheaply before Joyce began the reconstruction. Ali Asad, a Pakistani fast bowler with a first-class best of 9-74, proved demanding as Ireland slumped to 23-4 but Joyce and Johnston put on 122 before the Australian was bowled for 67. White and McCallan made useful runs and stayed with Joyce as he reached his second century in four days and was there on 115 when Mooney scrambled a single off the second last ball. Joy was unconfined as the squad realised that one win in the last two games - against the two weakest sides in the group – would be enough to claim one of the top five spots and a World Cup place.

The fourth game, against the USA at Waringstown, was abandoned without a ball bowled which meant one crucial point would have to be secured against Denmark at Upritchard Park, Bangor on 7 July. Form still hadn't returned to Molins, Bray and Botha, who were all back in the pavilion with the score on 28. Joyce again rode to the rescue with 60, and Gillespie made a gritty 40 before Dom Joyce flayed the bowling with a 37-ball fifty to see the score to 222. It was a great moment for the Trinity student who may have lived in his brother's long cricketing shadow – trials with Middlesex and Somerset didn't work out – but had established himself as the leading native batsman in Leinster.

If the batting had been conforming to a pattern, the opening bowlers were also happily in a groove. Johnston (3-39) and Mooney (2-22) blasted out the top order and White winkled out the tail. Jason Molins appreciated the significance of the achievement 'It is a huge day for Irish cricket. Playing in the World Cup will raise awareness of our sport in Ireland and hopefully spread it to a new audience. Making it to the World Cup was our number one objective but our goal now is to win the ICC Trophy.' Kyle McCallan, who that day became Ireland's most capped player told Ian Callender in the News Letter 'It's what I've been striving for the last eight years, when I went to my first ICC Trophy, and now, at last, I've a World Cup finals to aim for. I had a telephone call from Alan Lewis (the previous most-capped) congratulating me and that meant a lot.'

The opening rounds had been played north of the border and the knockout games were allocated to Dublin. This phase was anti-climactic, with four of the five slots for 2007 already filled (Ireland were joined by Bermuda, Scotland and Canada − and later by Holland), but Molins and Birrell believed the trophy itself was within their grasp. Ed Joyce was needed by Middlesex and thus missed the semi-final at Clontarf, but Gordon Cooke returned after missing the first week due to the birth of his daughter Chloe. Ireland broke through when Canada's John Davison was dismissed off the last ball of the fourth over, but unfortunately the total was on 46 at the time. Botha's mixture of pace and slower balls proved decisive as he took 4-47 and Canada were restricted to 238-9. Molins, batting like a man out of form, gritted his way to 44 but Ireland were only 106 when Botha was fifth out with 22 overs left. As had happened throughout the tournament, there were players to 'put up their hand' and Johnston (44) and Gillespie's stand of 65 turned the game back to Ireland. Gillespie (64*) scampered hard with White (28), who drove a six over long on in the last over to win the game by four wickets.

Joyce returned for the final, also at Castle Avenue, but skipper Molins was absent with a shoulder injury. Even though it was a Wednesday morning there was a huge crowd − estimated at over 3,500 − in time to see McCallan win the toss and Scotland put the Irish bowlers to the sword. Pinch-hitter Paul Hoffman knocked the Irish bowlers off their stride and Zimbabwean Ryan Watson made 94 as an enormous target of 324-8 was set. Dom Joyce and Morgan went early, but Bray clicked for the first time in making 70, and added 137 with Ed Joyce. The Middlesex man was batting well, scoring at a run a ball when he tried to flick a delivery from Scots captain Craig Wright onto the pavilion roof. It fell short and he was gone for 81, and with him Irish hopes of the trophy. They finished on 277-9 thanks to a record tenth wicket stand of 55 by Mooney and Cooke.

Although Molins or McCallan didn't get to lift the trophy, the tournament was a triumph for Irish cricket, and not just on the field of play where qualification meant a $500,000 bonus and one-day international status for four years. The tournament was very well organised, and the 26 grounds used looked and played all the better for the government and ICU grants ploughed into them. A legion of volunteers north and south ensured everything went off like clockwork, which was a great feather in the ICU's cap with the ICC.

The greatest prize, of course, was a place in the World Cup, the draw for which pits Ireland with Pakistan, Zimbabwe and the West Indies in a group to be staged in Jamaica. The fact that two of the three had been beaten in the previous two years gives Ireland hope that they can acquit themselves well.

Cricket is still a minority sport in Ireland, but with more than 12,000 players − two-thirds in Northern Ireland − it sits high up the middle order of participation sports. The reorganisation of 2001 also spawned a development plan part of which saw the appointment of a chief executive, Peter Thompson, formerly marketing director with Warwickshire. In the fourth century in which cricket has been played here, there are 246 grounds and 306 qualified coaches. Most activity is in the Northern area, with 50 clubs fielding 137 teams; Leinster has 40 clubs and 97 teams, North-West 27 clubs and

The Ireland team celebrate qualification for the 2007 World Cup after beating Denmark in Bangor. Back row: Ian Knox (physiotherapist), Peter Gillespie, Jeremy Bray, Trent Johnston, Paul Mooney, Kyle McCallan, Andre Botha, Dominick Joyce, Naseer Shaukat, Adi Birrell (coach); Front row: Ed Joyce, Andrew White, Adrian McCoubrey, Jason Molins, Gordon Cooke, Eoin Morgan, Matt Dwyer (assistant coach).

58 teams and Munster 21 clubs and 32 teams. In 2005, for the first time, a small league of five teams was played in Connaught, the boom in numbers chiefly due to an influx of players from cricketing countries.

This new wave of migration, like the first one that gave birth to the sport in the eighteenth century, has brought cricket to parts where it was virtually unknown. Clubs have sprung up in unlikely towns such as Ballyhaunis, Castlebar, Athlone and Shannon. If Ireland's recent successes can help these sparks into flames then the ancient game can go from strength to strength. Sabina Park is a long way from the Phoenix Park, and blue and green 'pyjamas' a far cry from the breeches and top-hats of Georgian Dublin. That journey which began in the Fifteen Acres doesn't end in the heat of Jamaica.

Forthcoming Titles Autumn/Winter 2005

Voices of Sport: We Are Rovers
EOGHAN RICE

Shamrock Rovers is Ireland's most successful football club and definitely the most recognisable of its soccer teams. It has an incredible record in terms of National League of Ireland titles and FAI cup victories. It has a considerable fan base regularly achieving attendance of 5-7,000 despite the fact that it has no fixed home-ground for the last few seasons while they await the completion of a new oft delayed stadium. Eoghan Rice is a journalist with the *Sunday Tribune*.

1-84588-510-4   €18.99

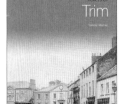

Voices of Trim
THOMAS MURRAY

Compiled by locally renowned author and historical Thomas Murray this book focuses on the life and times of Trim in the past centuries. With interviews ad stories from and about the town and its hinterland's unforgettable characters and events it is a charm for any native and a beautiful introduction for the visitor or new arrival. Featuring snapshots of the changing lives and lifestyles of a provincial town and with an unrivalled collection of old photographs to accompany the text it is bound to have a wide appeal.

1-84588-514-7   €17.99

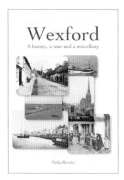

Wexford: History Guide & Miscellany
NICHOLAS ROSSITER

Nicholas Rossiter is a financial advisor working in Wexford. In his spare time he writes, produces and broadcasts a series of radio programs that combine Local History with Folk Music, a combination he find very effective and attracts contributions from across the world. He has been heavily involved in researching Wexford's History and has a considerable corpus of material at his disposal. Through this large body of material he takes the reader on a journey through Wexford's history and culture from early times to the present.

1-84588-528-7   €17.99

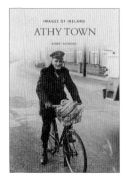

Images of Ireland: Athy Town
ROBERT REDMOND

Athy is a sizeable and fast developing town in County Kildare. It is a designated heritage town and has a rich history dating back to the 12th century. Robert Redmond is well established as a photographer in his town and has taken photos all over County Kildare and Athy in particular. There are wonderful and varied pictures featured in this book. Social, religious and sporting events are illustrated, not to mention, the people and picturesque landscape of Robert's much loved town.

1-84588-502-3   €16.99

If you are interested in publishing with Nonsuch Publishing please contact us at
Nonsuch Publishing, 73 Lower Leeson Street, Dublin 2

www.nonsuch-publishing.com